ARMED
&
DANGEROUS

THE PERFORMER'S GUIDE
TO DEALING WITH HECKLERS & INTERRUPTIONS

THIS BOOK CONTAINS SOME EXPLICIT LANGUAGE

JAMES BRANDON

ARMED & DANGEROUS

The Performer's Guide
To Dealing With Hecklers & Interruptions

By James Brandon

MORE INFORMATION IS AVAILABLE AT:

www.hecklertactics.com

©

Published by:

Invisible Inc.
Books

England

1st Edition 2011

ISBN

978-0-9569114-0-7

Contents

ARMED & DANGEROUS

THE PERFORMER'S GUIDE
TO DEALING WITH HECKLERS & INTERRUPTIONS

JAMES BRANDON

THIS BOOK CONTAINS SOME EXPLICIT LANGUAGE

WWW.HECKLERTACTICS.COM

WHY THIS BOOK PULLS NO PUNCHES...

The purpose of this book is two-fold. Firstly to give you the information you need to understand your enemy and secondly to arm you to defend yourself. Read that again, I chose the words very carefully.

The enemy we're talking about here is the enemy of interruption: Verbal and non-verbal.

Some of the material here is designed to help you deal with hecklers, some of it is to provide you with snappy answers to most situations you will encounter whilst on stage. Both have a common goal... To put you in charge.

When you are on stage you need to be in control: In control of yourself and in control of the room in which you are performing. If _you_ are not in control, human nature dictates that someone else is. You may be happy to work under those conditions and you are free to exercise your choice to do so, however, it does come at a price and with certain in-built pitfalls. More on those later.

This book is about taking control of a room from the various interruptions that a performer can face. In terms of the material contained herein, you will first learn to understand the nature of interruptions – deliberate and accidental, and know how to respond accordingly.

Please be aware that this book is designed for use in a number of different fields. The material contained herein is not for the casual observer. It is collated through years of experience and through the _need_ for such material. It is not collated because it is nice, fancy or clever. It is there to do a job so some, though not all, of what you will read here could be seen as harsh. If you've never been booked into a real tough venue then you can be forgiven for not fully understanding the inclusion of some of this material. That said, not _all_ the material in here is harsh – most of it isn't – But it's there if ever you need it. It is important to understand that all of the material in this book is usable.

If you think a line sounds too 'hack' or too harsh, then all that means is that it's not for you.

Rest assured that someone somewhere will need lines of that type to deal with the kinds of audience that they have to face and thank your lucky stars that it's not you.

Some lines will be of use to you, some won't, but they're all of use to someone, somewhere.

Now, let's face it, most performers would prefer to step out onto the stage without fear of interruption at all, but the real world can present an entirely different series of challenges to the ideology we dream about. Whether you're a pro, amateur or semi-pro, the chances are that you are going to get a tough crowd once in a while. The more shows you do and the broader the field that you do them in, the more your chances of a tough crowd increase.

ABOUT THIS BOOK

There have, of course, been hundreds of joke books over the years: Lists of put-downs, one-liners and gags of all kinds, although very few of them are written for professional entertainers. Those that do exist tend to be filled with jokes and quotations that aren't really much use to a professional.

The material is, nonetheless, out there: It's being used day-in day-out by professional entertainers. But as time has gone by something has slowly become apparent: Not much of it has been written down in one place.

That's what this book is about. It has been created as a reference on all forms of snappy answers and retorts for most of the situations that you are likely to encounter as a professional entertainer. It is by no means exhaustive and there's still plenty more to go at.

The material here has been carefully chosen for its real-world application. That is to say you can *really* use it in your everyday work. If you've ever read through a joke book and got more that half a dozen usable gags from it then you've done pretty well.

That's where this book is different... or at least that's where I *hope* it's different: It's full of usable stuff, dependent only on your style.

STOCK LINES

If you've been in the game for a while then some of this material will be well known to you. Some of it won't.

You may well think that you know who originated some of this stuff... So did I. In my research I have unearthed a few of surprises and also found plenty of people who claim to have created these stock lines.

It doesn't matter whether you're an 'old school' mainstream comic or an observational comedian, stock lines exist in every field. The lines contained in this book are in common use throughout the field of entertainment. So if you think I've included something that maybe I shouldn't have, do some research. You'll find that what you *think* is the 'original' source actually isn't. All the lines here are tried and tested.

Over the years I've heard plenty of comedians arguing about somebody else doing *'their'* joke only to find that *'their'* joke is in a hundred joke books. I know that because I've read a lot more than a hundred joke books. Anyhow, before deciding to sue me for including *'your'* joke, please bear in mind I'm not a wealthy man.

Now, a few things before we get to the good stuff...

Firstly, some of the material here is intended for the sharper end of the entertainment spectrum. The entertainers who work here are most likely to encounter situations where put-downs are necessary.

If you're easily offended then this book is not for you. It's not all politically-correct material, but then again it's not all offensive, blue & stag material either. It is intended for those who know how to choose and use their material and not all of it is intended for use in any one particular field. Some people will need strong put-downs, some won't.

Let's make a division here... There is a lot of discussion and argument in relation to what used to be called 'alternative' comedy versus old-fashioned 'mainstream' comedy. Stock lines exist in both fields. I have heard a lot of 'old-fashioned' stock lines being used by 'new school' performers. It seems that their appeal is universal. Many performers tend not to know *lots* of stock lines, so the same lines go around and quickly become over-used and then start to sound 'cheesy'.

If you know how to select, deliver and modify them, they shouldn't sound cheesy at all. If it sounds cheesy then you either chose the wrong line or you didn't deliver it correctly. Simple.

This book is not intended to be a book of original material (though some of it is), instead it is a book of material collated together for those that need it most: Working entertainers. It is for those who need snappy answers for the situations they encounter in the course of their work. It is not intended to be an original work of experimental material. By selecting the right line, modifying it to fit your purpose then delivering it in your own style you will be able to make stock lines work. It you get one of those phases wrong, they just won't work for you.

You may also find that some of the material doesn't read very well from the page. Most comedy is like that. If you don't believe me, write your act down and let somebody else read it out... See how many laughs it gets. Despite how it may read here, you can rest assured that all the material contained within these pages is broadly used, tried and tested.

To that end, some readers may find some of the material here somehow dated or old-fashioned. Some of it is! It's included because it works, not necessarily because it's new and unknown.

There is also a section which covers how to react in situations where comedy would be inappropriate. This advice is well worth studying, to make sure that you're aware of the appropriate response should you ever find yourself in one of these situations.

Additionally, it must be pointed out that I will mainly focus on *neutralising* the threat posed by hecklers and interruptions. The basic philosophy here is to shut the heckler up as quickly as possible and get back to your act. If you're looking to demonstrate an endless ability to out-heckle your heckler then the only route is to learn as many put-downs as you can. You'll find plenty of put-downs and snappy comebacks later in the book which you can learn at your leisure.

So, for those who prefer to neutralise interruptions and concentrate instead on their own material, read on, you'll be glad you took the time...

HOW TO USE THIS STUFF:

This whole thing started out as a list of gags and put-down lines. Then I began to realise that it would be foolhardy to publish a list of gags and put-downs without giving clear advice on how to use them. So here goes...

Put-downs are interesting things. They seem to be somehow urging us to use them at the first opportunity: To pick on some unsuspecting member of the public and give 'em both barrels for the slightest utterance and thereby establishing oneself as a leading exponent of staggering witty repartee. Used inappropriately put-downs and comebacks can be staggeringly *unfunny*, offensive and land you in a whole load of hot water.

In the coming pages we will discuss the use of this kind of material and how to understand the psychology of heckling and hecklers. That way you will always be justified in the use of a put-down, safe in the knowledge that you didn't just shoot from the lip.

CONTEXT

Using this material is all about *context*. It's all about using the right joke in the right context. For example: No-one in their right mind would want to insult someone about their personality, age or appearance – particularly a friend. That said, we might buy someone a funny birthday card that does just that, without a moments thought. Many of us have done that. But it doesn't cause offence. Why?

Context

The sender doesn't intend to cause offence and the recipient can take a joke. That's it. It was meant in the right way, you chose the subject matter carefully and delivered it in the right tone to the right person. Whether you thought about it or not it was a *considered* risk.

If you use the wrong joke on the wrong person it can be hurtful, embarrassing and unfunny. Done correctly, everyone's happy, so choose and use your material wisely. There are hundreds of lines to choose from in the 'Laughter Lines' section later in the book.

It is also important to point out that in the 'Laughter Lines' section I have duplicated some of the put-down lines from other sections. This is not to bulk out the book by using the same lines more than once, but instead to provide you with a quick and easy reference to all the lines that are relevant to a particular subject.

A line may cover two subjects so would need to be in two sections for easy reference and to save you from thumbing backwards and forwards to find all the jokes and lines on a particular subject. You may get fed up of seeing the same lines a few times, but in the long run it works in your favour, keeping all the relevant lines together for when you need them most. Counting the repeals there are almost 900 comic lines and put-downs in this book.

Please take time to read the early sections of the book which lay out the psychology of heckling and the types of heckle that you may encounter. A good knowledge of this may serve you very well in the future. There's a lot to consider: Justification, timing, tone of voice, delivery, subject... And lots more.

WHATEVER YOU DO, DON'T JUST WADE IN ARMED WITH A FEW PUT-DOWN LINES WITHOUT FULLY UNDERSTANDING THE RULES OF ENGAGEMENT

As the old saying goes...

IF YOU KNOW YOUR ENEMY AND YOU KNOW YOURSELF YOU WILL NOT BE IMPERILED IN A HUNDRED BATTLES.

ARE THEY REALLY ENEMIES?

In short... No. In fact the first interesting revelation is:

MOST HECKLES ARE FAIRLY WELL-INTENTIONED AND GOOD NATURED.

The real enemy is the enemy of interruption. That means anything that can cause your show to come off the rails if not handled correctly.

Surprising though it may seem, most of the time people will heckle you out of playfulness or in the spirit of 'joining in'. There is a misconception among audiences that entertainers – and particularly comedians – need 'a bit of banter' to enhance their act and spice up the evening's entertainment for everyone else.

The other popular misconception is that comedians do their own crowd control. More on that later...

The problem is that when we're on stage we feel so vulnerable that at times we can overreact. Add a bit of ego into the equation and you've got a volatile mix.

I once knew a guy who had two very conflicting character traits: He was painfully insecure and, at the same time, had a massive ego. Working with him was like waiting for a bomb to go off. It's similar to some performers when they find themselves under pressure. So the first lesson in all performing – and in particular dealing with hecklers – is...

STAY COOL

Bear in mind that you need to be in control. If you are going to be in control of the room that you're working – Be it a theatre or a truck-stop café – you first need to be in control of yourself.

If you find yourself in a position where someone in the audience is genuinely attempting to give you a hard time, then the audience need to see that you are unfettered by the interruption before you step up to put this d*ck-head away.

You'll understand why I put it in such terms when it happens to you.

Before we get to putting a heckler away – that's hitting them with just the right line - we must first be in a position to make an assessment of who they are and what their true purpose is. We must assess whether the heckle was just a light-hearted attempt to join in or whether it was a deliberate attempt to derail your show.

In order to make that assessment we must first understand the kinds of heckler we are likely to encounter, who they are and why they do what they are doing. It is only when we understand what is *actually* going on that we can really attempt to snuff it out with any degree of measurable success.

The following pages are designed to arm you with the correct tools to make the appropriate assessments, plan your counter attack and take it all in your stride.

ANATOMY OF A HECKLER

As I mentioned earlier, one of the most annoying things that any performer has to deal with is the misguided perception that some members of the audience actually think that they're *helping* by heckling a performer. I can't say with any certainty where the misconception comes from but there's no doubt it exists and so, in short, we're stuck with it. Why anyone would think that interrupting the flow of something somehow *improves* the flow is beyond me but nobody said this was going to follow any sort of logic.

So down to business...

Later we will look at some of the tougher types of heckler that you may encounter, but first of all I want to introduce the most common kind of heckler and the one we are likely to encounter more than any other. Ladies and Gentlemen, please welcome...

THE INNOCENT HECKLER

The *Innocent Heckler* is not to be confused with the more aggressive types of heckler that we will discuss later.

Now most performers are quite conversational in their style. They talk directly to the audience, often to individual members, and invite them to respond to questions and so on. It should come as no surprise, particularly if you're any good at it, that we conjure up the illusion that this is a two-way street... that it actually *is* a real conversation.

If you're connecting with an audience and they *like* you, they may come to feel that they *know* you. As a result they may then feel it's OK to join in. And why should we be surprised? After all, we created the ambience of *'friends in a conversation'* in the first place.

In this instance we have a couple of choices when dealing with hecklers and regaining control:

Firstly we may want to nip any conversational banter in the bud and reduce the likelihood of it happening again.

This would seem to be acceptable in the mind of a performer, after all it's *your* show and people paid to hear what *you* have to say.

But imagine the same scenario from the point of a spectator...

You created a convivial and conversational atmosphere, taking the audience into your confidence and sharing your musings with them, then you nailed them to the wall the moment they joined in. It all seems a bit heavy handed. Now if that's your style, then that's your style and if it works for you then there's no issue.

This book is all about understanding the different types and style of performer. There's material in here for everybody and this is not about any particular style having superiority over another.

That said, it takes a particular kind of performer to handle an audience in that way and it's certainly not for beginners or the faint-hearted.

The best way to handle the innocent heckler is also an important step in assessing whether it was an innocent heckle or not. The best way to deal with a heckler is:

IGNORE THE FIRST HECKLE

Ignoring the first heckle gives the heckler the opportunity to disappear quietly and cause you no further problems. The good news is that, most of the time, this is exactly what will happen. The heckler will realise he/she is not going to raise your blood pressure – Game over.

It is important also that you don't show any signs of being upset or shaken by the heckler.

Get into the habit of expecting the odd heckle here and there, this will help you to cope with it and to move on when it does eventually happen. Most of the time this expectation will be unfounded but it will help you to accept it as normal when one does come along.

You have to remember...

BEING HECKLED IS AN OCCUPATIONAL HAZZARD

It goes with the territory.

No matter how good you are you will be heckled at some point in your career. I guess you already know that, why else would you be reading this book? The trick is to know the score and to react appropriately.

It is important that you carry no fear when you enter the stage. You have to be relaxed when you perform. You have to be completely stress-free on stage in order to allow yourself to think clearly and, besides, being relaxed makes you look confident and super-cool.

There is no point in being *afraid* of a heckle coming your way. Being afraid certainly won't help your standing with the audience and it certainly won't prepare you to deal with any potential problems that may arise either. Instead we must learn to expect an occasional interruption and be prepared to laugh along with it and join in the fun now and again, particularly if you want the audience to accept what *you're* doing as 'a bit of fun' too. Yes, most heckles fall into the category of what the audience will see as 'a bit of fun'. Most of what you will encounter is well intentioned and no harm is intended. If you accept that and play along with it, you're half way there.

That doesn't mean that you let it all get out of hand and lose control over the audience, we're talking about the first heckle here. Give your audience the benefit of the doubt and follow the rest of the rules as we lay them out here.

Following the rules will significantly increase your chances of success against hecklers of all types. It will also provide you with the information you need to know which type of heckler you're facing and how to tell them apart.

WHAT CONSTITUTES A HECKLE?

When we're talking about heckles we're talking about the most common kinds of verbal interruption. We're not talking about specific events like someone dropping a tray of drinks in the middle of the dance floor, we're talking about verbal sounds, shouts from the audience, that kind of thing.

For the specific events you'll need to learn the appropriate responses so you can 'call' the moment. More on those later.

Remember that throughout this book we are going to cover all of the eventualities and interruptions that a performer can experience whilst on the stage. That means everything from a mild heckle to someone needing urgent medical attention, from people throwing things at you, to a full blown fight breaking out. I have experienced all of these along the way, some of them a number of times. Most performers are unlikely to encounter many of these eventualities as, thankfully they're quite rare but as the boy scouts say...

BE PREPARED

When (and if) these eventualities do happen to you, you'll be glad you took the time to read these pages. You will also add responses of your own to this collection. There will be things that happen along the way that will help you to be prepared for the next time it happens. **'ARMED AND DANGEROUS'** is all about having an answer for everything... And what to do when you don't.

But before all of that, back to our hecklers...

Now we've established that most heckles are harmless and friendly and we also know we've got to stay cool and take it in our stride. So far so good.

So how do we know that a heckler means business?

Well, in a nutshell, you'll find that ignoring the heckle just doesn't work and the interruptions continue.

We now need to bring in the second step of the process:

ASK THEM TO REPEAT IT

When ignoring them hasn't done the trick and the heckler continues to shout out, simply ask them to repeat what they said. Whether you heard or not, just ask them to repeat it as though you didn't hear.

I'll leave the choice of words up to you as these will vary from person to person, but they must be friendly and straightforward. You must not allow it to descend into 'fighting talk' with an abrupt 'you what'? It must be polite and friendly as though you didn't hear the first time.

What you're actually doing here is providing them with an opportunity to back down. The good news is that given the chance to back down, most people will take it. Don't be surprised if they disappear under the table or turn away from you in silence. Most hecklers don't have the bottle for a battle of words in public.

Whatever happens, make sure that if they do back down you are able to move straight on with your act, picking up where you left off. Don't make the mistake of labouring the point that they haven't repeated the heckle yet. Just allow them to back down and sieze the opportunity to carry on. This is the best way to avoid a battle of words and any further interruptions. Remember...

THE BEST ADVICE IF YOU DON'T FANCY THE PROSPECT OF BEING HECKLED AT ALL IS... DON'T OPEN A DIALOGUE WITH YOUR AUDIENCE.

If you really can't face the possibility that someone may shout something out during your show, then make sure that you arrange the content in such a way that you're not inviting them into a 'conversation'. Be aware though that excluding them in this way can come at a price.

You may miss a lot of opportunities for connecting with your audience and you may well find that you've got your work cut out to try and establish any kind of rapport with them. Nonetheless it is possible. A less Draconian solution is to avoid asking direct questions. There is little point in asking questions like:

'Are you all having a good time'?
'Anyone in from...'
'Anybody seen me before'?
'Where are you from'?

...and then being surprised when people start to join in later in your act.

Now if the innocent heckler *doesn't* disappear beneath the table you'll need the next phase of the operation...

THROW OUT A FEW MILD PUT-DOWNS

You'll find a whole section of these later in the book (in the section **'BE GENTLE WITH ME'**) .   You can pick the ones that suit you best, but for now you might say something like:

"Thanks for joining in, I bet your gob's happy when your asleep..." Or

"It's not her fault... When she was a baby her mother dropped her on her mouth"

If delivered in the right way, lines like these don't cause offence and they quickly re-assert you as the leader of the pack. Take time to learn a few mild put-downs from the later sections of the book, they'll stand you in good stead. Here is another important point...

YOU DON'T NEED AN ENDLESS LIST OF PUT-DOWNS IN YOUR HEAD. JUST HALF A DOZEN WILL SERVE YOU WELL AT FIRST.

Many performers have hundreds of lines in their head. All the lines you will read in this book are from memory, but I don't use them all. I only ever really use 6 or 8 on a regular basis, the others are just there if I need them. While we're on the subject let me let you in on another secret:

MANY PERFORMERS JUST CAN'T FIND THE RIGHT LINE WHEN THEY NEED IT MOST!

It happens to everyone. No matter how many snappy lines are inside your head, now and again your brain will let you down when you least want it to. This is part of the learning process. I can't tell you how many times a killer line has come to me *on the way home* from a gig. You spend the rest of the journey home kicking yourself over the fact that your brain didn't respond sooner. It happens.

The good news is that you will then commit the episode to memory and the line will be there for you the next time you find yourself in the same situation. It is nonetheless frustrating.

Another thing that you might want to do is to make up a cue card with brief reminders of your favourite put-downs written on. Many performers have these notes concealed on stage and refer to them when necessary. You can write out simple cue lines to remind you of a funny line in case you need it. If we were to make a cue sheet containing our two earlier examples we might write:

1. BET YOUR GOB'S HAPPY
2. DROPPED ON MOUTH

You can make these cue sheets as big or as small as you like.

One *very* well-known performer has his entire act (including put-downs) on cue sheets hidden all over the stage. He even has fake stage monitors that house the cue sheets so that the audience can't see them. Don't let anybody kid you that it's all spontaneous! He will, of course, take all the credit – and the huge fees – for his apparent brilliance and razor sharp repartee in dealing with hecklers, interruptions and having an uncanny ability to 'call the moment' (See page 52).

In the past I've used cue sheets the size of playing cards – in fact blank playing cards are good for this, you can buy them from most magic dealers. You can tape small cue sheets to mic stands, guitars, scenery, put them on the floor, whatever and wherever you wish. Just place them out of direct sight and off you go. I've also had cue sheets the size of A4 pages which I've just laid on the stage floor. I've seen people laminate A4 sheets to keep them beer-proof and once they arrived at the gig, lay them down on the stage.

One time I went to an audition, opened my briefcase to hand over my CV and photographs, then put the open case on the floor in front of the 'judges' table with my cue sheet inside facing me. I knew the act well, but it was just there as an *'aide-mémoire'* if needed. As it was below the table in front of them, they never knew it was there.

So, having the lines written down somewhere is not a bad thing at first.

I would recommend that you memorise them eventually, but you can write them down at first.

Just be creative about where you write your reminder... Write it down and tape it to your microphone, write it on the label of a bottle of water, the base of your mic stand, wherever. You'll soon learn the lines that work for you and then you can do away with the paperwork altogether. Magicians... Write brief cues on the side of a thumb tip and keep it in your pocket. Nobody will know they are there.

That's also a good tip, if you'll pardon the pun, for remembering the names of acts when you're a compére. For non magicians, thumb tips are also available from most magic dealers and, no, you don't need to know what magicians use them for.

It doesn't really matter where you put the cue sheet so long as the audience can't see it. The idea is that it acts as a quick reminder to jog your memory, it is not a full transcript of the gags. It is only a stop-gap. There is no substitute for knowing your material and that includes the 'ad libs' and put-downs you might want to use along the way. Learn them thoroughly and they will serve you well in due course.

Before we move on let's recap what we've learned so far:

- **BEING HECKLED IS AN OCCUPATIONAL HAZZARD**
- **BE PREPARED**
- **STAY COOL**
- **IGNORE THE FIRST HECKLE**
- **ASK THEM TO REPEAT IT**
- **USE A MILD PUT-DOWN OR TWO**

The above sequence makes up the primary drill for dealing with interruptions and hecklers. Whatever you do, wherever you go, whenever you encounter a heckler these are the steps that you will need to follow.

In 99% of cases you will find that if you follow the instructions above, you will be able to deal with the vast majority of the hecklers you meet without breaking a sweat.

It is important that you use the above 'drill' to make a fair assessment about your heckler. If you deviate from this 'drill' too much and start firing hard one-liners and put-downs at the first person to open their mouth, you may well come across as over-zealous and aggressive.

It is, however, possible to successfully build your style entirely around this principal if you choose to.

I have a friend who has the words *"Dare You Move?"* printed on his posters. He specialises in this kind of put-down and he excels at it. His audiences know what he does, they have come to expect it and that is what they come to see. It is also worth noting that he has over 35 years of experience in this field and didn't just step into it overnight after reading a book.

There are, of course, some more difficult hecklers around on the odd occasion. Some will be intent on giving you a hard time, others will be too drunk to notice. Regardless of the intent, you will need to be in a position to defend yourself, to regain control of the room and to know who you're dealing with.

Let's take a look at who else may be around to provide the unnecessary interruptions that can spoil your show...

TYPES OF HECKLER

So now we've got the basics out of the way, let's have a look at the kinds of heckler that we can encounter and the various ways of dealing with them. Remember that the *'innocent'* heckler is by far the most common heckler you are going to come across and they are relatively easy to deal with. Others take a little more work. Read on and let's see who's next on the agenda...

THE OPPORTUNIST

The *Opportunist* is sometimes referred to as a 'Hit & Run' heckler. He has a classification all his own due to the fact that it is difficult to tell why he/she heckles at all. The Opportunist is very similar to an *Innocent* heckler, but instead of being innocent he just lacks the bottle for any real confrontation.

The Opportunist will usually shout something out, intelligible or otherwise, then disappear the moment you respond. Generally speaking it's just a way of testing your mettle, but they never stick around long enough for us to really discover much more about them.

The method for dealing with an Opportunist is exactly as we laid out before...

- **IGNORE THE FIRST HECKLE**
- **ASK THEM TO REPEAT IT**
- **USE A MILD PUT-DOWN OR TWO**

That's it. After that they just disappear. If they don't disappear, then you're not dealing with an Opportunist. The only thing that really differentiates between an *Innocent* heckler and an *Opportunist* is that an Opportunist can shout rude, personal or aggressive comments.

The *Innocent* heckler is only ever playing around, albeit in the misguided belief he/she is actually helping you. The *Opportunist* can be mistaken for other more aggressive types of heckler, but it is important that you know that not all the unkind words that are ever shouted in your direction will ever lead to much. It would be easy to overreact to an offensive or personal-sounding heckle if we did not acknowledge the existence of the *Opportunist*. The Opportunist can pop his head up, shout his mouth off, then disappear the moment you respond.

The *Opportunist* is far from innocent, in fact he/she is usually *at least* a little bit naughty. It is only the fact that they hadn't banked on your ability to handle yourself against hecklers that dissuades them from becoming more persistent. That said, the *Opportunist* is not a real cause for concern due to the fact that they disappear so quickly. It is important, however, that you do not allow them to throw your train of thought. They are easily dealt with so make sure that you keep your cool and follow the first three steps as laid out on the previous page. The Opportunist will disappear at this point.

If he/she becomes more persistent then understand that you're not dealing with an *Opportunist*. The *Opportunist* will always disappear at the first sign of confrontation. They are the mildest form of 'real' heckler and as such they shouldn't trouble you too much.

Once you've followed the first few steps of the drill and they've failed to repeat the heckle you might say:

"Ah, a hit and run heckler! I was like that after my first pint..." or

"No school tomorrow, eh?" or

"Thanks mate, the bins are round the back..."

If they come back at you after one or two mild put-downs then the chances are that you're dealing with either a *Drunk*, a *Loudmouth* or one of the other kinds of heckler we can encounter.

For more information on these kinds of heckler and how to deal with them, read on...

THE DRUNK

OK before we go on, a quick point about drunk hecklers...

YOU CANNOT OUT-HECKLE A PERSISTANT DRUNK

The nature of someone who is *drunk* – not just someone who's had a drink or two – means that you cannot beat them with a battle of words. Sure, you'll get a few laughs but if they are so minded they just won't shut up and they'll eventually ruin the show. The power of logical thought has long since upped and left and they don't know whether they're this earth or Fuller's. They are also blissfully unaware of the fact that they're making an ass of themselves and spoiling the evening for everyone else, but this is a factor that you can turn to your advantage.

To deal with a drunk the best method is to follow the first three steps of the drill again to assess who you're dealing with. That's...

- ## IGNORE THE FIRST HECKLE
- ## ASK THEM TO REPEAT IT
- ## USE A MILD PUT-DOWN OR TWO

By this time you'll know what you're up against. Next, hit them with a couple of '*drunk*' lines.

You might say...

"Last week someone threw a petrol bomb through the window. Before it could go off, he drank it" Or...

"I've told you before... You shouldn't drink on an empty head"

...and stuff like that. There are many suitable lines later, I choose these just to illustrate the point.

If the drunk becomes persistent then make the smart move and put the whole episode to bed as soon as possible. Once you realise they're drunk, they're not simply going to go away and they're going to ruin the show for everyone else, you might say something like:

"Ladies and Gentlemen my job is to entertain <u>all</u> the people in the room tonight. I've tried to deal with him in a fun and inoffensive way so that I can get on with my show for everyone else. As this guy seems intent on spoiling the evening for everyone else all I can do is ignore him and get on with the show for everyone else, if that's OK with you".

Pause here as you'll most likely get a round of applause.

You're also likely to turn the rest of the audience against the offending drunk and they'll most probably get on his case and shut him up for you. All you have to do then is do exactly as you said you would – *Get on with it and ignore him*. This takes quite a bit of concentration but the situation usually corrects itself quickly, leaving you to get on with what you came to do.

If it doesn't correct itself then all is not lost. It just takes a little more extreme action which we'll discuss later. The method for dealing with a persistent heckler is exactly the same as dealing with a drunk heckler only the drunk is much less likely to know it's time to shut up, due to the fact that he has lost the full use of most of his senses.

If at any time you find yourself unable to get on with your act because of a persistent heckler, use the above speech to shut them up. *Persistent* hecklers and *Drunk* hecklers are from the same mould.

It is important that you don't mistake someone who's just had a few drinks for a drunk heckler. What we are talking about is someone who is so drunk that they have lost the power of rational thought. Someone who has just had 'one too many' is unlikely to cause you any *real* problems if handled correctly. A *drunk* will cause you nothing *but* problems. A few drinks will loosen the tongues of most people and dull the senses to a degree. For most people that means they will:

1. Talk louder than normal.
2. Have a little 'Dutch courage' that they normally wouldn't have.
3. Be unable to respond quite as rapidly as they might like to .

This also means that while they'll be a bit louder and more confident than normal they'll usually still have the presence of mind to shut up and not spoil the evening for everyone else.

Conversely, the true *Drunk* is unlikely to be aware of how others in the room are reacting. In any case, it is worth noting that in the case of the drunk heckler – and for that matter any heckler you may encounter...

AT NO TIME SHOULD YOU LOSE YOUR TEMPER OR SHOW SIGNS OF AGGRESSION TOWARDS A HECKLER

The more drunk the heckler is the more unpredictable and volatile they can be. Note also that your *'I'm here to entertain everybody...'* speech was not directed towards the drunk but instead it was directed towards the rest of the audience. The purpose of this is to get as many people on your side as possible and let *them* do the work for you. Remember, the chances are that some of the audience will know the offending drunk and will be able to talk him/her down for you.

If the situation ever begins to get out of hand make sure you adopt one of the **'EXTREME MEASURES'** described later in the book. All of these approaches will work for you and - rare though they are - they are all situations that I have encountered over the years. It is not necessary to soldier-on with your act in the face of overwhelming and extreme circumstances.

You may also find that the heckler may change from one type to another... A drunk guy may go from being a drunk heckler to an aggressive heckler and so will need to change your course of action.

Now it is important that we pause for a moment. All this talk of drunks and aggression may have frightened a few of you. Please be aware that ...

SITUATIONS LIKE THESE ARE RARE

You may encounter them only once or twice in a career, and the chances are, if you're lucky, you may never encounter them at all. I mention them only so that you are prepared if ever you do.

Making sure that you are prepared for such eventualities will only allow your confidence to build and this will show in your on-stage persona.

A lot of this kind of confidence comes from a mixture of knowing you're well prepared and having the experience to know that what you're going to do actually works. It's also a bit of a Catch 22 situation... You need confidence to make it work and it works only because you have the confidence to do it.

Nowadays most comedians enter the comedy world directly through the thankless arena of 'Open Mic' nights. Most old-school comedians entered the business indirectly. They were either singers or musicians or some other kind of performer who slowly transitioned their way into comedy by adding a few gags to their musical act until the comedy took over and the music disappeared. There are exceptions. That said, whatever your route into comedy there can be no substitute for good old-fashioned experience.

This is the greatest teacher of all and it is where most of your confidence will come from. In a nutshell...

WISDOM CAN BE TAUGHT, LESSONS CAN BE LEARNED
BUT EXPERIENCE HAS TO BE GONE-THROUGH

That's enough philosophy for now. Let's have a look at who we might next encounter on our travels...

THE PREPARED HECKLER

There is a special kind of heckler that has emerged in recent years. They have their own 'stock line' in their head, solely for the purpose of hitting back at a comedian should the need arise. They usually reside in venues that have a regular program of comedians and have evolved in response to entertainers who base their act on picking on certain members of the audience. It is important to note that some entertainers do this very successfully and without causing any offence to their 'victims'.

In some cases the prepared heckler has evolved because some 'genius' of an architect has located the public toilets so near to the stage that every time anyone needs to use them they have to walk in front of the stage to do so.   Under the circumstances, what's a comedian to do?

If the audience know that each time they pass the stage they're going to get a skitty comment from the on-stage comedian, then the chances are they'll prepare an answer beforehand, just to even things up a little.

The prepared heckler can, on occasions, deliver a *killer* line so, as an entertainer, beware who you pick on and make sure you're prepared for a comeback where required.   I'll give you an example...   The comedian is on stage when someone walks past towards the toilets.

The comedian says something like: **'Where do you think you're going'?**

The prepared heckler would reply with something like: **'Sorry mate, I'm just off for a p*ss before the comedian comes on'.**

Where do you go from there?   Well, the comedian might reply with something equally acidic like:

'Well mention my name and you'll get a good seat... I'll get you on the way back...   It'll be the longest p*ss you've ever had...'.

Yes, it's an acidic remark and no, it's not polite, but such is the nature of *some* of the work you may encounter.

It is also important to note that you must retain the element of fun in your voice if you choose to deliver lines like these. Your tone must give out the message that the heckler *has* got one over on you, you're taking it in good fun, but you're having the last word all the same.

When he eventually comes back to his seat you needn't say anything at all if you don't want to. Just a nod in his direction will get a laugh. If you want to deliver your own killer line here, you'll win. Most prepared hecklers only have the one line and once it's gone, it's gone. That leaves the opportunity to reassert yourself as the 'leader of the pack' wide open if you choose to do so.

Remember that our earlier rule still applies here: If you don't want to get into a dialogue with a heckler you could simply ignore the person walking past and get on with your show. In my opinion, the best advice is to *only* tackle the necessary hurdles.

YOU SHOULD ONLY INTERRUPT YOUR FLOW FOR AN UNAVOIDABLE OUTSIDE INTERRUPTION THAT EVERYONE IS AWARE OF

Deliberately interrupting your own show to do a put-down is more work than you actually need and, from an audience's point of view, can appear to be a bit heavy-handed. There are exceptions, though these depend on your style and experience.

Other well-known lines you may encounter from a prepared heckler include things like:

You: *'Can you hear me at the back'?*
Them: *'Yes but I'll swap with someone who can't'*

You: *'Have you seen me before'?*
Them: *'I wouldn't have turned up tonight if I had'*

You get the idea.

If the put-down examples on the previous page are a little too strong for your style then you can act out a playful acceptance of *'knowing when you're beaten'*. It's a good way of preparing for the unexpected without having to think on your feet or to remember a specific line.

In doing this you are also acknowledging the fact that the heckler has got one over on you but you're doing so in a comic way and accepting it in the spirit of fun.

To illustrate, you might say something like...

"I'll give you that one...
(Under your breath) ...You b*stard.

Despite how it reads on paper, the delivery must be playful, and not aggressive. And, OK, you might want to substitute the expletive if it doesn't suit your style or your clientèle, but the message remains the same. You might instead say...

"I'll give you that one...
(Under your breath) ...Smart alec.

...or whatever suits your style, but make sure you say it funny, not aggressively or disparagingly. Keep it humorous and good-natured and you'll get a laugh... And you'll keep the audience's respect (and control of the room) too.

The real art in dealing with the *Prepared Heckler* lies in your ability to laugh at yourself. If you can take a joke then this will endear you to the rest of your audience. If you laugh *with* them you'll win. There's nothing to stop you 'nailing them to the wall' after you've neutralised their line by laughing along.

A *'false corpse'* may help here too. *'Corpsing'* is the act of laughing unintentionally when you're on stage. A *'false corpse'* is when you *act* like they made you laugh as though it's unexpectedly caught you off-guard and broken your stride. Many entertainers use this ploy as it looks both gracious and spontaneous to an unsuspecting audience.

It is equally important that you don't go too far with all this good-natured stuff. After all, you don't want to create the illusion that the heckler is the star of the show and is funnier than you. The fact is that they won't be, they'll only have the one funny line and once that's out, it's over to you. At least, I hope that's true. Just don't expect *them* to know it automatically.

You'll need to help them out here... Acknowledge the joke then just follow up with a few mild put-downs and you'll be back in control. You need to demonstrate that while they got a laugh, you're the professional here and you're in charge. Remember too that if you don't laugh *with* them, you'll run the risk of looking beaten and bitter. You might have been beaten, but only for a moment.

You might then say...

"Right, that's enough from you. We've all laughed at your joke and you're too bloody funny... Now p*ss off.

Again, despite how it reads, the tone here is *playful* and in the spirit of fun, regaining control in the process. You can exchange the actual words to suit your style and your clientèle.

Along a similar theme you might say...

"Right that's enough of that. There could be a copyright problem here, I'm supposed to be the funny one. Let's pretend it's my show for a moment, shall we"?

Again, no matter what you choose to say here, make sure it's in the spirit of fun. That is central to making this technique work and saving you from looking like a complete loser in the face of a funny line from someone in the audience.

In short you're trying to get a laugh from something *you* didn't say. Make sure you're smart enough to give credit for the heckler's line and then add to the laughter yourself. If you are at the centre of it and you can add to the laughter you can claim all the benefit (and some of the credit) for yourself. Just make sure you look gracious while doing so. After all, you're basking in reflected glory here.

As with our similar situations, play along, keep it fun and upbeat, deal with the situation and most important of all...

GET BACK TO YOUR ACT AS SOON AS YOU CAN!

I can't stress enough just how important this is. It is another key component in the process of looking confident and at ease on stage. Your act is the focal point of your time on stage and it is *this* material that you are most familiar with.

MAKE SURE YOU KNOW WHERE YOU'RE GOING NEXT

When dealing with interruptions of any kind you must make sure that you know where you're going to go next. If you stopped mid-flow, make sure you've remembered where you left off, then pick up from there when the interruption is over. Forgetting where you're going next will only serve to hammer another nail into your performing coffin If you look flustered as you attempt to regain your place after an interruption. It just looks wrong. Stay cool, take it all in your stride and keep yourself focused on what comes next. This way you can pause, deal comfortably with the interruption and get back to the action. That is, after all, what you came to do.

If the heckler attempts to become part of the act after his first successful heckle you will need to put the episode to bed quickly. The best way is to wait for them to heckle again and ask them to repeat it, just as before. This time their heckle line will be pale by comparison, nobody is that lucky. You can then say:

"The first one was good but that was a 3 out of 10. If I was you I'd have quit while I was ahead". Or:

"You tell all the jokes you like, there's only me getting paid for it..."

You can then use any other put-downs you like to further control the situation. Again, if they fail to shut up you'll need to be familiar with how to deal with persistent hecklers and be able to structure your comeback accordingly.

THE FUNNY GUY

The Funny Guy is someone who we might usually refer to as 'Bar Funny'. The term 'bar funny' applies to someone who is the 'life and soul of the party', the joker in the pack, the class clown, but *not* a professional comedian. These people are referred to as 'bar' funny because they are normally funny around the bar over a few drinks with friends – but that's where the humour begins and ends. Getting up on stage and doing the same thing is far beyond his/her capabilities, but among friends over a few drinks this guy is king. They often don't know that it takes a whole load more to get up on stage and create the same hilarity among a group of complete strangers.

It is the ignorance of this knowledge that can lead the *Funny Guy* to be a disruptive force within the room, especially if this is coupled with a few drinks and a bit of encouragement from his mates.

Tackling the *Funny Guy* goes one of two ways. As always the golden rule is to ignore the first heckle, if the interruption becomes persistent ask him to repeat the line, then use one or two mild put-downs. So you might say something like:

"I normally do this bit on my own, but thanks for joining in..." or:

"Thank you, mate. Let's pretend it's my show for a minute, shall we?"

A gentle reminder that you're in control is usually enough.

The second way that the *'Funny Guy'* can go, is that he/she cracks a joke that only the group around him/her can hear. They'll roar laughing and cause everyone else in the room to look at them, but nobody else can hear the joke. Remember you are the only one with a microphone here...

You might simply say:

"They're making their own jokes up over there, that's saved me a job"

or:

"They're making their own jokes up over there. I'm only sorry that I didn't bring microphones for everybody..."

And that is usually enough. The object is to get back to the act you were booked to perform as soon as you can.

Though it can be deeply gratifying, it is not always necessary to 'nail a heckler to the wall'. Just do as much as you need to in order to neutralise their threat and then move on. Like we said before, it is your *act* that everyone came to see and *that* will be the material that you are most familiar with. Don't work any harder than you have to by coming off the script. If you're off the script then any weaknesses will soon begin to show. Just deal with the idiots only as far as you have to and then get back to the script. One thing is for certain...

THEY WON'T PAY YOU ANY MORE MONEY
FOR DEALING WITH HECKLERS

It is your ACT that they're paying for. OK, if a heckler gets in the way you'll have to deal with him/her, but only do enough to get them out of the way, then get back to the good stuff.

If the *'Funny Guy'* later turns into a *'Loudmouth'* or a *'Persistent heckler'* then you'll need to adapt your approach to deal with them.

To help familiarise you with the approaches, let's have a look at how *'The Loudmouth'* operates...

THE LOUDMOUTH

You've probably realised by now that hecklers are much-of-a-muchness: They all do pretty much the same things and the responses required to deal with them are pretty similar too, it's just that some are more extreme than others... So are the methods for dealing with them.

The only real difference between the different types of heckler is how quickly you can shut them up and the techniques you'll require to do it.

The general idea when dealing with hecklers is to do so without genuinely causing offence. We will later discuss the issue of 'insults' when dealing with interruptions and hecklers. Before we discuss the use of 'insults' let's understand who is going to be the biggest recipient of this kind of put-down.

'The Loudmouth' is the one you'll probably have the most fun/trouble with on a regular basis. Like we've said, the *Innocent* heckler is the most common and they rarely cause too much of a problem. *The Loudmouth* is the most common of the 'real' hecklers.

The Loudmouth is exactly as the name suggests. He's going to be the one who talks loudest and you'll hear them over everybody else. Depending on your venue, you'll hear them in the bar, they'll talk during your act, during the bingo, the auction, the raffle, during the speeches, in fact anywhere they can draw attention to themselves – appropriate or otherwise. The good news, as far as we're concerned, is that the *Loudmouth* will always lead with his/her chin. They'll walk head-long into a put-down without a moment's thought. There's an old saying that goes:

EMPTY VESSELS MAKE THE MOST NOISE

...and The *Loudmouth* is no exception. They usually have very little to say but make a lot of noise saying it. Their motivation is not usually jealousy but instead born out of the desire to be heard.

To that effect they are fairly easy to deal with, mainly because they don't have the arsenal of put-downs and comebacks that you have. All that is required is a cool head and a reasonable stack of put-downs.

If you can target the put-downs to hit where it hurts, the *Loudmouth* will be powerless to fire back.

Occasionally the *Loudmouth* will attempt one or two comebacks but will quickly just run out of steam. The real technique required on your part will be to stay cool and make sure that you look completely unruffled by their attempts to have the last word.

The Loudmouth can often come at you with a few sideways requests... You'll be mid-flow at the beginning of your act and the *Loudmouth* might say something weird like: *"I say, mate, do you sing any Country and Western songs"?* Or something else totally irrelevant. They may make a comment about your clothing or your appearance, all in an attempt to throw your concentration. Another factor is that the interruption often comes In the form of a question.

Understand that the question is actually irrelevant and is only designed to derail your train of thought. Remember this...

HE WHO ASKS THE QUESTIONS ALSO HOLDS THE POWER

The actual question and it's content is usually irrelevant. It can be something like: *"Where did you get your shoes from"?* Or something equally pointless, but remember that it's not *what* the question is that's the issue here. The issue is *who* is answering the questions. If the *Loudmouth* can get you answering the questions, then *they* are in control... And that's where the trouble begins.

IN ORDER TO DEAL WITH THE LOUDMOUTH, MAKE SURE THAT YOU NEVER ANSWER ANY QUESTION ASKED OF YOU

The *Loudmouth* is attempting to undermine you. If you answer the question here you are taking the first steps on the slippery slope to entering a dialogue on their terms.

Make sure that instead of answering the question that you fire one back. It's a really simple process and is equally easy to remember. So the dialogue between you might go something like this:

Him: *"Why have you got a tie on"?*
You: *"A heckler! What's your name, mate"?*

You are now, in that one simple phrase, making the first move towards regaining control. The *Loudmouth* will often make a name up here, it doesn't matter. Who cares what his name is? Whatever the answer is ask *'Where are you from'?* Or any other question that you can bring to mind.

The point of all this is to establish the convention that the heckler is answering *your* questions. Ask two or three questions here, it doesn't matter what they are, or for that matter what the answers are. There are two major points to this exercise:

1   You regain control
2   You get some thinking time

The heckler will usually drop out of the questioning process early, but judge for yourself when you want to move to the next stage. Once you're ready you can skim out a few put-downs. You can use almost any line that fits but you'll look a lot stronger if you hit them with something that's particularly relevant. You might say something about them being a loudmouth...

"Do you make this much noise when you're having sex?   Can't remember that far back, eh"?

Or for a female heckler...

"Do you make this much noise when you're having sex? No? Quick somebody sh*g (hump) her"!

There are hundreds of lines, you'll find them later in the book and can choose one that suits your style. I use these just to illustrate the point. You can also use the *'insults'* section if you prefer to use a more barbed but relevant comment.

Make sure you read the separate section on *'Insults'* and make sure you know exactly how to use them. While they are called *'insults'* they are not designed to actually insult anybody. Read the section on their use carefully and make sure you fully understand what is required before attempting to put them into action.

The purpose of using 'insults' is to pick a relevant characteristic from your heckler and focus on that. While they *are* stock lines, it should appear that they are spontaneous ad-libs. The more person-specific the lines appear to be, the more effective they will be for you.

Again, it is important to recap that the primary drill should be put into action before any of this takes place. At the danger of repeating myself once too often the primary steps are...

- ## IGNORE THE FIRST HECKLE
- ## ASK THEM TO REPEAT IT
- ## USE A MILD PUT-DOWN OR TWO

After this the *Loudmouth* will make him/herself known. If they don't begin asking stupid questions, they'll interrupt you or you'll just hear them being overly-loud while you're trying to work. You can then just follow the same 'questioning' process mentioned earlier to establish that you are in control.

Once they have answered a couple of questions – remember the answers are irrelevant – you can move onto a couple of put-downs. You might say:

"I'm sorry was I talking when you were? How rude of me..."

It doesn't matter which put-downs you use, just make sure they're relevant and they suit your style. The more relevant they are, the more funny they'll be.

THE DISINTERESTED LOUDMOUTH

The *Disinterested Loudmouth* is a variant on the *Loudmouth* as we have come to know him/her. The *Disinterested Loudmouth* is the person in the room who, instead of heckling you directly, will be having a conversation at an absurdly loud volume while you're working. In doing so, they are showing a deliberate disregard or disrespect for what you're doing and for anyone else who may be watching you.

They will be holding court among a small number of the audience and generally getting in the way of the focus of the rest of the audience.

You should always begin by politely asking them to shut up and allow you get on with you show. A simple:

"Keep the noise down will you, I'm trying to work here..."

...is enough to let them know what you want them to do. If – and only if – they become persistently noisy, then here's a great technique for dealing with them... Learn it carefully and it will work well for you. In order for it to work correctly you must make sure a number of essential things are in place first:

1. **You are in rapport with the rest of your audience.**
2. **That you speak directly to the heckler.**
3. **You then turn your attention back to the rest of the room to ask the questions that follow.**
4. **The delivery is pacey.**
5. **You keep it clear and polite.**

Let's imagine you have someone standing at the bar holding a really loud conversation while you're on stage. By now you will have already followed the first three steps of the drill and you will by now have established that this interruption isn't just going to go away by itself. The noise will just go on and on (and get louder) if allowed to.

If it becomes a major disruption, stop what you're doing and say this...

"Hang on a minute..."

Then speak directly to the heckler, turning quickly back to the rest of the audience where appropriate. Pace is everything here.

"Hang on a minute. (To Heckler) Answer me a question, how many rooms are there in this club/pub/bar/hall?"

They may or may not know the answer, it doesn't matter. Keep the pace up here, this is not a slow questioning process, in fact going too slow can sound patronising and will be counter-productive.

If they say a number then you can proceed with the following speech if they say *"I don't know"* just modify it accordingly. You might say:

"Four? Well but I'm trying to work here. I realise that you might not be interested in what I'm doing, but (TURN TO THE REST OF THE ROOM HERE) I reckon there might be one or two other people in the room that might be... (THE AUDIENCE WILL USUALLY APPLAUD HERE, THEN TURN HALF-WAY BACK TO THE HECKLER)... I don't want to ruin your conversation but how about having it in one of the other rooms here so I can entertain everybody else here, seeing as this is the only room with a stage?"

At this point someone may well begin applauding.

If, when you ask how many rooms there are, the heckler says: *"I don't know"*. You can say:

"Neither do I... But I'm trying to work here..." and then continue with the rest of the speech from there.

As long-winded as this sounds, if done correctly and at the right moment it really works. Remember this is not a speech to deliver to the first person that opens their mouth, *they have to be perceived as a persistent problem by everyone in the room* before you're able to use this successfully. The key point of the statement is to get everyone else in the room on your side and get them to add *their* support to *your* point and shut the heckler up. The heckler is much more likely to take heed if he/she knows that the rest of the room is against them too.

Next... GET BACK ON WITH THE ACT! No pause for thought, no waiting for the heckler to leave, just get on with it and make sure you pick up where you left off. The heckler will usually either leave or just go quiet.

A word of warning... This speech is not useful for shutting up a room full of people. It works only in a situation where a small group of people or an individual are spoiling the show for everyone else. It should only be used as a last resort and with good cause. It relies on the rest of the room helping you to shut up a smaller group of others by adding *their* weight to *your* point. For advice on how to approach shutting up a room full of people, take a look at the section **'SHUTTING THEM UP'** later in the book.

Over the years I have found this approach to be particularly useful when someone who has missed the start of the show makes a loud late entrance, showing no regard for what's going on.   You can lose the room completely when someone does this. When their interruption becomes disruptive to everyone else in the room, you can usually be justified to use the technique. Don't use it at the first opportunity, it isn't necessary or justified. If you do it right, other members of the audience will congratulate you on how well you handled the noisy interruption. If you get it wrong you will look moody and heavy-handed. Make sure you're justified, comfortable and confident with it before taking it on. If you haven't got all the requirements in place before attempting it you will come unstuck, so make sure you know what's required first. Recap the five requirements I laid out on page 42 – They are essential.

Remember also that a *Disinterested Loudmouth* can often have descended into the habit of disrupting the same room over a long period of time. They are often 'regulars' at a particular venue and can persistently disrupt the acts in the same venue over a long period. Once you step up and shut them up, or provide the opportunity for the rest of the audience to vent their own frustration at them, the others may well thank you for providing the opportunity to do just that. They may have come to dislike the interruptions just as much as you do.

The *Disinterested Loudmouth* is not usually prepared for a comeback and so will either leave quietly or shut up under pressure from you and the rest of the audience. Again, make sure that you're prepared in case they don't. A few extra put-downs will suffice.

Bear in mind that this technique is not effective where the majority rule is against you: The majority of the people are making the noise and the minority are wanting to listen.   Under such circumstances any success will be limited. They will either shut up for a moment then start talking again, or not shut up at all and you will lose your credibility.

Remember that we should not show any signs of anger or irritation when dealing with them.

The key to success is always staying cool. Showing signs of anger and irritation means that the fun is over and the heckler is getting to you. The audience will be uneasy with that and laughs will be hard to get.

THE CHILD HECKLER

In the arena of live entertainment there can be few things that are harder to handle well than child hecklers. I have heard many stories of people attempting to silence them and in doing so taking on far more than they can handle. Kids entertainers can do it as it's all in their persona, but for comics and other entertainers it can be a tricky area. The best advice here is to leave child hecklers alone and work on the parents instead. If the child becomes a pain in the ass, then the real secret is to embarrass the parents into taking action on your behalf.

A bit of interaction with a child isn't going to bother you too much but a persistent child heckler is another matter. As an adult, if you take on a child heckler you're going to look unkind and unfunny. Nobody will laugh if you really put a child down, although you can try a few lines about them to the rest of the audience. You might say something like:

"I've got a superglue lollipop in the car..." or lines like that.

The following skit is also useful in bringing an end to a dialogue with a child: Ask the child their name and a few more basic questions like: Where do you live, age, etc. Then ask: *"You know when Daddy goes to work and Mummy's in the house on her own... Does anyone else come round to the house?"* Kids often answer 'yes' without understanding the further connotations. You can then say *"We'll draw a discrete veil over that one then shall we?"*. And move on... An embarrassed mum will soon come and collect her little darling.

If a child is persistently disruptive you can embarrass the parents into action by saying something like: *"If I was one of your parents I would be embarrassed at the way you're behaving"*. Beyond this there is little you can do with an unruly child. Whatever you do, don't go full-on into a string of put-downs. The audience will turn against you in no time.

As you grasp the techniques and become more assured about how to deal with hecklers and interruptions you'll quickly become more confident in your ability to cope with them without breaking a sweat. It is at this stage that the confidence will not only begin to grow, it will begin to radiate from you...

...And that is powerful, my friends.

THE PRO HECKLER

This is really about being heckled by another act or entertainer. As unlikely as it sounds I've seen this happen at entertainment showcases, talent nights and in one case a full-out gala show. It's when the on-stage performer is heckled by another performer(s) from their vantage point in the audience. It's all about ruining *your* performance and making *themselves* look good.

There are two ways to deal with this situation. The first one is to hit them with a few well timed put-downs, the same as you would for any heckler. The only addition I would make is to give them an introduction first so that the entire room knows that you're being heckled by a fellow 'pro'. Remember that most people will consider it unspeakably rude to heckle a fellow performer so the majority will be on your side to begin with anyway.

When you spot what's going on you can quickly stop what you're doing, change tack and give the *'Pro'* heckler an introduction...

"It's so nice to be heckled by a fellow professional. Ladies and gentlemen will you please welcome (Joe Bloggs)..."

The audience may or may not applaud here. Both reactions work in your favour. If they applaud they are following your instructions, if they don't it's probably because they don't want to applaud the idiot. Now you can follow up with whatever put-down line you like. Bear in mind that although *he* might be a pro and may have heard the line before the rest of the audience won't. You also have another thing in your favour which he doesn't...

...A microphone.

The second way of dealing with pro hecklers is to embarrass them into silence. This takes a bit more bottle and a super-cool demeanor to do, but if you can muster the courage and handle it well, it will work for you.

It works particularly well if your first approach fails to silence him, so you may wish to look upon it as a second option – i.e. Try the other one first.

This technique brings the show to a complete standstill so make sure you only attempt it if you know you're strong enough to pick up where you left off without looking shaken. If it looks like the experience has shaken you then you will lose the audience and the exercise is counter-productive.

The technique is similar to the one we used for the Persistent or 'Loudmouth' heckler. However, there are a couple of variations and approaches that you can employ here. They're both similar in style and they both work well, it just depends on your style...

An old ruse is to say something like:

"Ladies and Gentlemen I know that some performers have a list of put-downs that they use for situations like this. I didn't reckon on ever being heckled by a fellow professional so I don't have any. We'll settle this by way of applause... Applaud now if you want to listen to him (pause)... Applaud now if you'd rather listen to me (pause)..."

The audience will be on your side.

I know, I know, I can hear you... *'But what if they're not?'*

If the audience indicate that they'd rather listen to him than listen to you, then the answer is...

There's something wrong with your act.

Either your act isn't worth listening to or you've been booked in the wrong kind of venue for your type of act. This happens now and again – being booked in the wrong venue, that is. The golden rule here is to make sure that the audience is on your side *before* you attempt it.

IF YOU ARE BEING PERSISTENTLY HECKLED ON A REGULAR BASIS, IT'S TIME TO TAKE ANOTHER LOOK AT YOUR ACT.

Bear in mind that pro hecklers are rare, nonetheless they do exist. You will find that by-and-large the audience will be on your side and will want to hear what you've got to say. They will be unhappy about any kind of interruption, particularly if it's a deliberate attempt to derail your show and ruin the evening's entertainment for them.

KEEPING YOUR COOL

As with all put-downs, the key ingredient is the coolness of your demeanor and your delivery. Staying cool is absolutely fundamental to your success and this is *particularly* true when dealing with pro hecklers. The audience will always remember just how cool and calm you were when facing such an interruption. It is the sign of a true professional.

Remember to re-word the 'pro' heckler statement to suit your own style. It is a very extreme step to take so you should only use it in extreme circumstances. You should have learned by now that in all instances of dealing with hecklers the first steps are:

- ## IGNORE THE FIRST HECKLE
- ## ASK THEM TO REPEAT IT
- ## USE A MILD PUT-DOWN OR TWO

If that doesn't do the trick then we need to begin to assess which kind of heckler we're dealing with. Once you've worked out that it's a persistent pro heckler who is intent on ruining your show and isn't going to stop, then more extreme measures are required. You can rest assured in the knowledge that the audience will be on your side and, if you know what you're doing, it's not too difficult to deal with.

It is important to note that despite all the discussion here, dealing with most hecklers is usually down to the observing the three points above. After you've followed those points, most hecklers are over and out.

99% of the time the heckler will back down at the first opportunity leaving you to get on with your show. It is only when they become a persistent problem that any real effort is required.

Use the information laid out here to assess which type of heckler you're actually dealing with and then just follow the instructions. Always ensure that you are confident in your ability to deal with each situation before attempting to do so publicly.

It is also important to know, particularly if you're using put-downs for the first time, that the *delivery* of your line is paramount.

There will be lots of different types of performer reading this book because hecklers affect most performers from time to time. That makes it difficult to give clear advice here on what will be the correct approach for <u>you</u> under a particular set of circumstances.

So, for those who haven't had to deal with this kind of stuff before it is firstly important to point out that you shouldn't rush the delivery of your put-down lines. Part of the 'staying cool' process is in the delivery of your comeback line... Or any comic line for that matter.

Most comics fear silence. To the newcomer, the fear of silence can be so overwhelming that it can throw your timing completely. Much could be written about the subject of timing but for the purposes of this book let's just look at a bit of simple easy to remember advice about timing put-downs. In simple terms here it is...

Make sure that when you deliver a put-down line you don't rush it. Take your time, stay cool and say every word carefully. This way there's less chance you'll trip over the words and screw it up. Nothing will kill your kudos more than tripping over a put-down.

The most common mistake is to rush because you think you've got to be fast in your response. Just take your time and if the audience can hear every word, your chances of success are increased enormously.

There is, of course, a lot more than just that to the subject of timing. I have assumed that you already have a good grasp of comic timing and the idea here is to give a bit of quick advice on timing put-downs.

In many cases it can work best if you say the line to the audience rather than the heckler himself. You may need to modify a put-down line to do this. It is usually just a matter of changing a word or two, like changing the word 'you' to 'he' and then delivering the line indirectly by talking <u>about</u> your heckler rather than <u>to</u> your heckler. Remember too that saying the lines too quickly or skimming over certain words can spoil the little bit of magic that a one-liner contains so be cautious with your editing. In time you will learn to chop and change them, but for starters just take your time. It will pay you dividends in the long run.

CONFIDENCE IS KING

I have said that staying cool is probably the most vital ingredient in the put-down game, and it is. The question then has to be 'where does this confidence come from'?

Confidence is a strange animal. I'm not sure that confidence can be learned from a book, although it is certainly a *learned* phenomenon. What I mean is, as small children, we all start out confident. Running around naked or throwing a loud tantrum in public seems not to bother us. Later, through a series of conditioning events in our lives, the confidence is steadily knocked out of us.

For performers, our lack of confidence is usually encapsulated in one or more of these three statements:

1. **'I'm not as good as everybody else'**
2. **'Something might go wrong'**
3. **'The audience won't like me'.**

That's about it. Suffice to say that you need your confidence to be in peak condition before attempting to tackle hecklers.

If your confidence *is* at something of a low then the best thing you can do is... *Rehearse.* I know it sounds too simple to be true – perhaps even a little boring – but that's the truth. The better you know your material, the more comfortable you're going to feel about performing it. As you rehearse make sure that you're asking yourself *'what will I do if that goes wrong'* or *'what will I say if that doesn't work'?* This self-questioning exercise alone will build your confidence to new levels. The knowledge of having a way out or a prepared response for all eventualities will, in itself, allow your confidence to grow.

It is worth noting that in many ways you won't actually *feel* your confidence grow. You'll just find that, in time, you'll begin to worry less, sleep better and have fewer tough shows.

From a personal point of view I don't ever recall becoming confident. I do remember being afraid of telling jokes or, to be precise, failing to get laughs, but I don't recall actually *becoming* confident.

Gaining confidence is a gradual process... And, like growing older or gaining weight, it's so gradual that you don't feel it happening. It is, nonetheless, happening.

I recall once working a show where the audience was full of other performers. When the show was over a guy came over and said "*I tell you something, you haven't got an ounce of fear in your body*". I was a bit surprised and asked him what he meant. He said: "*You walked onto that stage like you had a mortgage on it*". It was a moment of realisation. I realised that I was just getting on with what I do, not really phased by who was in the audience. The confidence he spoke of was there without me knowing it. To him it looked like boundless confidence. To me, it was all about knowing what I was doing and knowing that it would work. I hadn't contemplated anything else. Gaining confidence had been such a gradual process that I didn't know much about it, It was someone else who actually brought it to my attention. That's how it is.

If you fear going on stage, or that things may go wrong then the best advice is always...

REHEARSE, REHEARSE, REHEARSE

Nothing is going to prepare you better for dealing with interruptions than knowing your act inside out. You need to be in a position to have your mouth continue to do your act while your brain works out the most appropriate response to an interruption. Weird though it sounds, this kind of multi-tasking is common amongst comedians. It is developed by extensive rehearsal and performance of your material.

Once you completely know what you're doing with your material, your brain is free to search out those killer put-downs you require. It is also able to keep the act going at the same time. If this sounds impossible, then think about how we can drive a car without really thinking about it. Our minds wander but we are still able to drive. Sometimes we can read a page in a book while thinking about something else. Our eyes may follow the words but our brain is elsewhere and it is only when we reach the bottom of the page that we realise we weren't actually taking it all in. You've probably already done it while reading this book. You can easily turn this kind of multi-tasking to your advantage.

CALLING THE MOMENT

When a specific mishap occurs while you're on stage you'll want a killer line to pull the focus back to you. A dropped tray of drinks, a mobile phone, a stray laugh, someone walking across the stage... They will all happen to you at some point. Having a great comeback is all part of gaining kudos as a master of witty repartee.

It is known as 'calling the moment' and the only way you're going to get it is by memorising the appropriate lines. Sorry to disappoint you...

The good news is that all the responses you'll need are in the **'LAUGHTER LINES'** section later in the book. Take time to study them and commit them to memory, they will serve you well in time.

Through your use of put-downs and snappy replies you will give the impression that you are *ad-libbing* as you go along. That is the nature of most ad-libbing. It is the application of a relevant stock line to a situation, or the *modification* of a stock line to fit a situation. Occasionally someone will genuinely ad-lib a killer line, but it's rare.

Ad libs are usually based on prepared (stock) lines that are quickly edited to fit the circumstances. To be able to edit quickly you have to be very familiar with the material, so make sure that you take time to study it well. A thorough knowledge of it will stand you in good stead for many years. A knowledge of stock lines also matures with age and you'll get better at recalling them over time.

The creation of *genuine* ad-libs is all about stripping down to the core of the issue. When somebody shouts something about, lets say, your hairstyle, then the core issue is either 'fashion' or 'appearance'. Hair is a subsection within either of those topics. Now you can take a look at the heckler's fashion or appearance and use that as a basis for an ad-lib. Personally I think it's better, to begin with, just to put-down 'across' them instead.

To put-down 'across' someone you completely *ignore* the issue they're alluding to and instead do a line about them being a loudmouth, being a nuisance, being a drunk, or something like that. So, to illustrate, the dialogue might go something like...

Them: *'Who cut your hair'?* (or whatever they shout out)

You: *'Ah, this guy thinks he's a wit... And as it happens he's half right. Thank you for joining in mate, I'll take it from here if that's ok with you'.*

OK it's not the best choice of line but you can see what's happening: The heckler is trying to draw you in one direction with his question on hair and you're cutting across them with your response in another direction. You are removing the heckler's ability to ask questions simply by not answering them. You're just putting his interruption to bed by disregarding it and putting *him* down instead.

This is an extension of our earlier point about not answering a heckler's questions. Later you may feel confident enough to handle questions on the-hoof, coming up with your own genuine ad-lib answers based on the core of the question (in this case 'hair') but it is not for the faint-hearted and certainly not a subject for beginners.

As a starting point for learning how to *'call the moment'* read through the *'situations'* section later on in the book. Write down the lines which appeal to you, making sure that you have all eventualities covered. You'll need just one line for each situation at first so pick the one that suits you best. Now you will have a list of snappy lines to cover you for all eventualities. In doing his you have narrowed your focus and reduced the number of lines you have to learn. You can learn more and add them to your arsenal later.

There is no easy way to do the next bit... You've got to learn them. You might want to make up an audio file on your computer or mobile phone by recording the lines as you say them, play them back and then learn them that way. You can then burn them onto CD if you prefer, or just learn them by writing them down in a good old-fashioned notebook. However you choose to learn them, you need to have them committed to memory and ready for use when called upon.

A good arsenal of situational comebacks can elevate your status with an audience enormously and can stand you in good stead over many years. Take time to learn suitable lines and you'll always be prepared.

INSULTS

We have already discussed the importance of *context* and the need for a playful tone of voice in the delivery of certain lines. The subject of *'insults'* demonstrates just how important this kind of delivery is.

When we speak of *insults* we're talking about the kind of put-downs that hit hecklers where it hurts. Whilst we refer to them as insults, we're not really talking about insults per se, instead we are talking about the kind of comebacks and put-downs that send a warning shot across the boughs to let a heckler know that we're not afraid to shoot from the lip. It also lets a heckler know that while they're firing the insults that we too can return the fire, with interest. The insult put-down is designed to expose a particular character trait or physical attribute of the heckler and cause other members of the audience to laugh at that. It can be highly effective in the right hands.

In reality, the act of genuinely insulting a member of the audience and *really* causing offence is the probably the worst thing you can do. There are some notable exceptions. If the audience is completely on your side and a heckler is getting on *everyone's* nerves, nobody will blame you if you nail the heckler with a suitably barbed witty insult. In such circumstances you can proceed, safe in the knowledge that he started it and it will be observed by all present that he got what he deserved. However, a decent level of proficiency at kick-boxing usually adds to the completeness of the preparations.

Many comedians have made a good living solely out of taking the mickey out of members of the audience using stock lines. By and large, audiences seem to lap it up but, for the purposes of a book about dealing with interruptions, we will say that we only use these kind of mickey-taking put-down lines if provoked.

This way you know that *they* started it and you're only defending yourself. That said, the same lines could be used for merciless unprovoked mickey-taking if that's your thing. Let's not make judgements here, it's either funny or it's not and your audience will tell you that.

In the coming pages you will find lines for every kind of physical attribute you can think of: Tall, short, thin, fat, bald, hairy, the list goes on... There are also lines about personal qualities: Lazy, drunk, etc. The important thing now is that you know *how* to use them competently.

I remember once being heckled in a club in Bradford. There was a guy in the front row who was mouthing off and generally getting in the way of the act. After following the usual procedures I hit him with a few mild put-downs - to little or no effect. He became louder and more personal so after a while – and noticing he was bald – I said:

"By the way mate, who parted your hair, Moses?"

It's a stock line and there are many others like it. The result was that it got a big laugh from everyone else in the room and after that, the heckler promptly shut up.

After the show I was in the dressing room, the door flew open and there was the heckler coming towards me. I was confused for a moment, trying to work out what he might do next.

In a heartbeat he outstretched his hand, grabbed mine and shook it. *"Well done, lad"* he said. *"I'll give yer that one, yer wa' good"*. In short I'd earned his respect through my ability to come back at him and shut him up on his own turf... But think of the consequences if I hadn't handled it very well. The guy clearly had no fear of confrontation, he merely opened the dressing room door and walked in. If I had upset him he would have just been more compelled to come in and settle the score. It was only the delivery which had let him know that I was only having a gentle go back and not just spoiling for a fight or being intentionally malicious by *'insulting'* him in front of his mates.

Remember that it is very difficult to put across the tone and manner of delivery by just writing down stock lines. You must be absolutely clear that you can deliver the line in just the right manner before you ever contemplate doing so for real. So, the lesson is this:

MAKE SURE THAT YOU ARE ONLY EVER LAUGHING WITH AND NEVER AT A HECKLER

Remember that most times a heckler will be heckling you in the spirit of fun, not in anger. Make sure that you respond in kind and that you do not cause genuine offence. This is the 'birthday card' humour I mentioned earlier.

To recap, 'birthday card' humour, as the name suggests, is the kind of joke you find in greetings cards. You know the kind, they contain mild jokey insults that you might send to a friend for a bit of fun. Step into a gift shop and look at the cards on offer, you'll find many examples of the 'socially acceptable insult'. They usually joke about how old someone is, how they drink too much or how they fancy themselves as a bit of a ladies man, this kind of thing. They don't cause offence because of the context in which they are used.

There are, of course, always exceptions to the rule and some very experienced comedians can get away with things what many of us might consider to be fairly heavy duty stuff. For example, in recent years I've heard a few comics use the line:

"I know it's rude to ask a lady her age so... How much do you weigh'?

It is important to note that you should not attempt to use a line like that without a full knowledge of what's required. Use such lines with appropriate caution and due trepidation. You should...

NEVER ATTEMPT TO COPY THE STYLE OF A STRONG COMIC WITHOUT A FULL UNDERSTANDING OF WHAT'S INVOLVED

A strong comic will spend years developing his style and his on-stage persona. When you see that comic work, it will look very easy to do what he does. It isn't.

It looks easy because the comedian *makes* it look easy. This happens because he has spent years developing and learning his craft. He/she will be in absolute rapport with the audience. They will have made many mistakes along the way and will have become a stronger act as a result. What you see on the stage is the result of many years of study, hard graft... And failure. Don't underestimate it.

If you attempt to deliver the same 'killer' lines as he does, without the full understanding that the comic has developed, you will potentially crash and burn on a galactic scale.

LEAVE THE STRONG STUFF UNTIL YOU KNOW YOU ARE TRULY READY FOR IT

Even though the comic may use some fairly strong material, the same rules still apply – It's all about *context*.

These kinds of comedian have often built their popularity through their ability to deliver quick, barbed one-liners and unprovoked put-downs. That is precisely why their audiences like them and why they pay to see them. I know some of these kind of comedians and despite what some may think, they're no idiots. They have found their audience and give them exactly what they want. They usually hold the theory that if people don't like them, then they shouldn't go along to see them.

It is also important to note that in the spirit of 'diversity', all audiences have an equal right to their own particular taste in entertainment. It is pointless to imply that only one kind of comedy really counts and that all others are just too 'hack' or outdated. Such opinions do exist but what entertains a middle class audience at a £20-a-head comedy club is unlikely to have the same effect on a working class audience in a club on a tough council estate. Both styles must co-exist as they serve a common purpose in diverse circumstances. They are both designed to entertain their respective audiences. That's all.

Every genre has its fashions and comedy is no exception. It is true that 'insult' comics seem to have fallen down the pecking order in recent years and they have more than their fare share of critics. Conversely it is also true that they have their fare share of supporters. By its very nature, 'insult' comedy, it seems, will always divide opinion.

You can make 'insult' jokes work for you as long as you fully understand the rules of engagement. The context must be absolutely clear and the recipient – or at least the rest of the room – must be on your side. Approach 'insult' comedy in the same way that two friends might banter with each other. Keep it playful and upbeat and you should be on reasonably safe ground.

At an event, I remember once using the line:

"Earlier today a car pulled up with a jerk, the jerk got out and here he is!"

Now if I tell you that the person I used the line on was the President of The Entertainment Agent's Association of Great Britain you might spot the potential for causing offence.

The truth is that I know him very well, so the context was right, the audience laughed and he laughed too. It sounded like two friends enjoying a bit of banter because that is exactly what it was. However, we should not ignore the reality that if I had got it wrong it would have been a total calamity and I could have lost a lot of work as a result.

This balance of context, tone and delivery is what 'insult' comedy is all about. If we had to give this subject a definition we could say...

PUT-DOWNS ARE PLAYFUL 'INSULTS' THAT ARE GIVEN AND RECEIVED IN THE CONTEXT OF FUN

It is important that you don't just wait until after you've said the line and then add a cursory: *"I'm only joking"* on the end. It just won't wash. It will look like you're backing down and if you're delivering a strong message and want to hold the audience, you can't afford to look like you're backing down. You will just lose the audience there and then if you do.

It is vitally important that the comedy element in any 'insult' line is clear. If you make the comedy element clearer than the 'insult' element then there's less chance of causing any genuine offence with the line. It also means that the recipient is able to accept it in the spirit of fun. If you focus instead on the insult context of the line you will primarily convey that and therefore run the risk of causing offence.

'Insults' can play for big laughs if delivered correctly and it is worth taking the time to understand them fully. If you study them well and use them appropriately they will add a considerable force to your comedy arsenal.

SHUTTING THEM UP

If there's one thing that will happen to you more than any other it will be the eventuality of working in a noisy room. This is where you walk onto the stage and everyone just keeps on talking. It mainly happens where the entertainment is free or when the on-stage performer is not the 'main event'.

When I first started doing stand-up it was the one thing I couldn't seem to fathom out. I asked around among other comics who were all very non-committal about how they handled noisy rooms and how they dealt with people who wouldn't shut up and give them a chance.

Then one guy, a very well established tough comic, said to me:

"I'll tell you how you do it... Go on and do your act and if you're any good they'll shut up and listen".

It seemed like tough advice at the time, but there's a lot of truth in it.

The best advice on handling noisy rooms is: Follow all the other advice you've read so far, it's all part of the same package...

WHAT REALLY SILENCES AN AUDIENCE IS A PERFORMER WHO LOOKS LIKE THEY KNOW WHAT THEY'RE DOING AND LOOKS LIKE THEY'VE GOT SOMETHING TO SAY.

I know that seems like a cop-out, but it's true. Make sure that you walk onto the stage confidently and get on with it, no messing. Make sure that the audience feel compelled to watch and pay their full attention to you.

I have tried a number of other approaches with varying degrees of success. If a room is *unbelievably* noisy you can just stand there and wait. It will feel like forever as you wait but it can be very effective. Again, this is not for the faint-hearted. In fact most of the methods for dealing with noisy audiences require a good dollop of courage to make them work.

After all you are about to take a large group of people and, single handedly, tell them all to shut up.

UNDER NO CIRCUMSTANCES SHOULD YOU EVER LOSE YOUR COOL OR START TO LOOK DESPERATE

Never beg your audience to be quiet or start talking to them like some irate school Headmistress. That *will* get them laughing at you – and for all the wrong reasons. Instead, stay cool and show them that you're prepared wait for their attention.

One technique that's really effective is just to stand and 'shush' them down. It sounds simple, perhaps even a little patronising, but it seems that the 'Shhh' sound is universally accepted as the the noise we make when we want people to shut up. The oddity is that it actually seems to work.

You might want to try stopping mid-flow and just remind them that you need them to be quiet. You can do this by making the *'shhh'* sound whilst motioning with your hands that you want them to calm down.

Another option is to make a simple 'be quiet' statement. It might be something as simple as:

"Ladies and Gentlemen I just need a little quiet up here"

Any kind of statement like this will usually work if delivered in a polite but firm manner. As always you will need to get back to your act, picking up where you left off as soon as you can.

So what happens if they *don't* shut up and the problem persists? Well, the action you need to take all depends on how extreme the situation is...

In the most extreme of circumstances you might not be able to get on with your act at all. On occasions a room can be so noisy and hostile that it's impossible to go on. Once in a while you may find yourself at one of these kinds of nightmare gigs...

If you do find yourself standing on stage in a situation like this you need to take evasive action quickly. If you need to get off stage, you might just say, firmly:

"It looks like you're not ready for me, give me a shout when you're ready and I'll come back and do my act".

Then get off stage. Again the tone of your delivery is important. Despite how it may read, the delivery must be clear, self-assured and assertive, not wimpy and apologetic. Say it and get off.

This approach is only for use in a situation where you have completely lost control of the order in the room.

If the room is really hostile then it's time to consider your personal safety. Refer to the **'EXTREME MEASURES'** section later in the book for further guidance.

It is important that the tone of delivery is firm but friendly. I have done this a few times on some really tough gigs and under extreme circumstances. However, please remember this is an extreme course of action and only for use when an audience is totally ignoring you.

Even though it is a rare occurrence, it can happen and you need to know what your options are before you're faced with the dilemma for real. For those of you who may want to say 'the show must go on...' and other assorted fables, you must understand where this will lead you under such extreme circumstances.

It is possible, should you choose, to perform your act while nobody listens, while everyone talks and order in the room is lost. In most circumstances the crowd will just get louder and if you keep going their indifference can turn into irritation. That irritation can later turn into anger and that anger can turn into hate and you really don't want to be around when the audience hate you, so learn to take a hint. In most cases it won't escalate to this, but it can. Nightmare gigs are rare, but I have seen it happen on occasions.

The other option is that they forget you're there and you end up talking to yourself. Neither outcome is going to do you any favours.

One of the key skills to surviving nightmare gigs is to know when you're beaten. It may well not be your fault that you're getting such a reaction from them (more on that later) but as the old saying goes...

IF YOU CAN'T WIN, AT LEAST DON'T LOSE !

One of the popular misconceptions about comedians is that they do their own crowd control. This is not part of the deal and it certainly won't form part of your contract. As a performer you are entitled to a reasonable 'orderly' atmosphere in the room that you are working. That means that if the people organising the debacle haven't got that in place for you, wait until they have.

On subjects like this there will always be a lot of conflicting advice around. It is important to remember that much of the 'show must go on' type of advice you may hear will come from those who have very little experience of these situations in the real world. If someone is only doing a few shows a year, or only working in a certain environment, then they will not understand that situations like these could ever present themselves for real. In tougher venues they can and they do, but in more upmarket venues they are rare

Most of the time the show will 'go on' and you'll enjoy happy audiences and good shows which will be free from interruptions and be fun to perform. This book is all about what to do when things don't go exactly as planned. Putting all that information in one place at the same time can make it all sound a bit daunting and make it appear that bad events are an everyday occurrence... They aren't. The important issue here is that you understand...

IT IS NOT NECESSARY TO STAND AND PERFORM UNDER EXTREME CIRCUMSTANCES OR WHERE YOUR PERSONAL SAFETY MAY BE IN QUESTION.

So to recap the 'noisy audiences' dilemma...

First try 'shushing' them down by making the 'shhh' sound and motioning them to calm down with your hands.

Next you might try a firm but simple verbal statement like:

"Ladies and Gentlemen I need a little bit of quiet here..."

But overall it is your act that is going to silence them more than anything else. A good counter-attack on the noisy room is to really 'press on' with your act, keeping the pace up and exaggerating the speech. Make it compelling to watch and you can win them over despite the odds. You can only do this is you have at least some of the people paying attention to you.

If all else fails then you may have to accept that you're just not the right act for them on the night.

Later, in the **'EXTREME MEASURES'** section we will examine all you need to know about 'dying' on stage, how to deal with hostile and unruly audiences and how, if you're struggling, it might not all be your fault.

Before we do all that it's time to pause for a moment.

I sincerely hope that the information you have read so far has not scared you away too much. Instead I want it to help you to prepare for any eventualities that lie ahead and to give you the confidence to neutralise them before they could ever get out of hand.

Understanding the nature of interruptions will put you way ahead of the game when it comes to counteracting them. Armed with this knowledge you should soon be performing more confidently and taking it all in your stride.

Under extreme circumstances you will be able to ensure that the show can successfully 'go on' and have the know-how to deal with it when it can't.

AND NOW IT'S TIME TO REVISE...

Before charging head-long into using the various lines that follow you will need to revise everything that we have covered so far.

To save you the time and trouble of reading the last 60 pages again you may have noticed that I have written all the key information in bold capitals. When you're ready, go back to the beginning of the book and skim each page for the big bold type. These are all the key points you need to know, brush up on these and you're half way there. If you do want to read the first section of the book again then that will stand you in *really* good stead and also ensure that you more fully understand what is required. The choice is yours. I would recommend a complete re-read but I understand if you can't be bothered. Just read the stuff in big bold letters again.

Whatever you do, make sure you understand each point *fully* and that there are no grey areas for you. You must know *exactly* what is required before attempting to do any of this stuff for real.

The book is also intended to be used as an ongoing reference for you. Keep it in your suit bag, take it in the dressing room with you, keep it in the glove box in your car, you never know one day it may save your bacon. There is also space at the back of the book for you to write notes and any new lines you come up with.

The next section of the book contains all the put-down lines and comebacks you'll need. As you read through the lines in the following pages mark out all the gags that fit your style.

The last section of the book is entitled **'EXTREME MEASURES'** and is designed to give you the information that you won't find anywhere else. This section is dedicated to giving clear instructions on how to deal with some of the most extreme circumstances that you may ever have to deal with while on stage.

They have all happened to me in the past and I pass on the information to you to enable you to deal with the situations appropriately if ever they do occur when you're on stage.

LAUGHTER LINES...

COMIC LINES AND COMEBACKS
FOR ALL TYPES OF INTERRUPTION

BE GENTLE WITH ME...

Let's begin with a few gentle put-downs and build up from there. In the pages that follow you will find some general put-downs then a load of more specific lines for dealing with most situations you'll encounter.

Use the stronger stuff with caution. I have included stronger lines only for those who know how and where to use them. You can cause some serious offence and get yourself in a whole load of hot water if you get these wrong. Remember, you were warned!

SOME LINES ARE REPEATED IN THIS SECTION. THIS IS NOT DONE TO BULK OUT THE BOOK, RATHER IT IS DONE BECAUSE SOME LINES ARE RELEVANT TO MORE THAN ONE SUBJECT. IT ALLOWS US TO PUT ALL THE RELEVANT LINES IN EACH RELEVANT SECTION AND SAVES YOU HAVING TO SKIP BACKWARDS AND FORWARDS TO FIND WHAT YOU NEED. SORRY IF YOU GET FED UP WITH READING ANY REPEATS, JUST COUNT IT AS REVISION (!)

So let's picture the scene... You're on stage, busy doing your act and your first heckler steps up to give you a hard time. First you ignore them, then you ask them to repeat the heckle, then all you need is a couple of mild put-down lines to shut them up. Let's begin with...

Thanks for joining in, mate. I'm going to a drugs party afterwards. You can come if you like, I've got to take my own 'dope'...

Sit back in your chair and we'll plug it in.

You know, you shouldn't drink on an empty head.

Keep shouting mate... It's not that I enjoy listening to you, it's so that Security can see where you're sitting.

I'd like to help you out. Which way did you come in?

This man believes he's a wit and as it happens, he's half right.

I thought alcoholics were supposed to be anonymous.

Listen, if I want your opinion I'll give it to you.

There are some things in life that go without saying. Would you mind being one of them?

No, seriously, it's nice to have you with us... Will you be staying long?

Yes mate, keep taking the tablets...

Yes mate, anyway thank your mother for the rabbit.

I've seen you on television... Interference.

Where are you from? (Reply) I'm sorry? (Reply again) Yes I heard you, I'm just sorry...

I was playing in a gay club last night and I've got to say it's a coincidence seeing you twice in one week!

I've listened to your humble opinion and it has every right to be.

I can see you have a ready wit. Will you let me know when it's ready?

(Two hecklers) There they are – Dumb and Dumber (or Tweedle Dumb and Tweedle Dumber)

He's not a complete idiot. There are still some parts missing.

You have all the makings of a perfect stranger.

Thank you! I used to know a funny version of that joke.

(Ask them to repeat the heckle then let it fall to silence..) You see, it's not easy, comedy, is it?

(Ask them to repeat the heckle) Do you see that? Every time I move my foot, his mouth works!

What's on your mind? If you'll pardon the exaggeration?

You know, you ought to be on TV. At least that way we could turn you off.

Who said that? Come on give us a wave... I'm not gay, I'm just friendly. Oh! He looks disappointed!

There's never a dull moment with him. It's continuous.

Wahey! No school tomorrow, eh?

I was like that after my first pint.

Do up your flies, your brain's hanging out.

There he is... Living proof that Snow White and Dopey did have sex.

I see you're getting turned-on down there... So is your wife.

The bins are round the back, mate!

Earlier on this evening a car pulled up with a jerk. The jerk got out... and here he is!

Sorry mate, my leg has just gone to sleep. Mind if I join it?

He doesn't have a lot to say. Unfortunately you have to listen for quite a while to find that out.

He was born on the 2nd of April. A day too late.

Yes mate, it's never too late to have a happy childhood.

Rumour has it that he's just had a charisma bypass operation.

Thank you for giving us the benefit of your inexperience.

Thank you for joining in. Twenty years I've been doing this and now he decides I need a partner! Not only that but he thinks it should be him!

Put your hat on there's a Woodpecker flying about.

(Bald heckler) Crikey! I'm being heckled by a Genie

That's my motto... If you can't get a laugh, start a fight!

Here's a guy with something to say for himself. Even his neighbours threw a brick through his window just so they could hear him better.

They all talk loud in his family. They had to, there was no lock on the toilet.

His wife's sold the piano and bought him a clarinet. He can't talk while he's playing the clarinet.

How would you feel if I came round to your house and interrupted while you were performing?

I'll come round where you work tomorrow and knock the bin off your back.

Are you heckling me or just practicing all the words you know?

I'm sorry, I couldn't hear you, I was talking...

I'm sorry, was I talking when you were? How rude of me...

I'm sorry I didn't bring microphones for everyone

Here we go, the charge of the light-ale brigade.

Nice to see liquor mortis has set in.

Did you pay to get in? Have a look on your ticket. Is your name on there...anywhere? No! That's because I'm the one that supposed to be doing the talking!

If you were the one they came to hear don't you think that all the seats would be facing you?

I bet your gob's happy when you're asleep.

Sorry? (Repeat) Yes I heard you, I'm just sorry.

Every village has one... Here's yours.

Is this your first time as a heckler?

I'd love to stop and chat but I'm a bit busy right now...

Do you join in when you go watch a movie?

Why don't you shut up and pretend we're playing bingo?

Thank you mate, I normally do this on my own but thanks for joining in...

I'm sorry I didn't realise it was your turn to talk.

I bet you can't swim... You can't keep your mouth shut long enough.

He is arguably one of the best thinkers in the country. Apparently he's still arguing about that.

We could do the show in his mouth, there would be a bit more room.

She reminds me of the Venus De Milo. Nice to look at, but not all there...

I've seen you on television... Crimewatch (Most Wanted).

(LET THE ROOM FALL SILENT) Do you hear that silence? You made that!

Sit next to the wall that's plastered as well.

STRONGER STUFF

His family tree is a cactus. They're all pr*cks.

He's only grown a moustache so he can look like his mother.

Opinions are like as*h*les. Everybody has one but we don't necessarily want to hear it.

Do you have a chip on your shoulder or is that just your head?

I bet his family tree has no branches.

He loves himself so much that when he has an orgasm he shouts his own name!

If I gave you a match would you go and find a gas leak?

You should put a condom on your head. If you're going to act like a d*ck you should at least dress like one.

If I wanted to listen to an as*h*le I would have farted.

I wish I'd have known this was going to be a heckling contest. I would have checked my brains in at reception and we could have started even!

I wish your neck had a number on it... I'd ring it.

Did you know that last week the government sent a letter to all the people in (PLACE) with an IQ above 10? Do you know what it said? No? Well there you go...

I don't mind being heckled, but it's my brother. We don't normally speak but you never know when you're going to need a kidney. To you out there he might be just a d*ckhead but to me he's a bone marrow match.

Why pick on me? You were so gentle in the toilets half an hour ago...

There are two things I like about you... Your face.

You should sell yourself to a ventriloquist.

If your d*ck was as big as your mouth maybe you'd be sat there with a girlfriend tonight.

Save your breath for your inflatable girlfriend when you get home.

Do you know what I like about you? F*ck all!

Who lit the fuse on your Tampax?

He's a clever guy! His brother is at University. He's in a jar in the Biology lab.

This is what happens when cousins marry!

She has everything a man could want... A beard, moustache, hairy chest, big muscles

Please welcome a lady who has just returned from entertaining the troops... One at a time!

You've got a good head on your shoulders. Of course it would look better on your neck...

What are you going to do for a mouth when Moby Dick (Free Willy) wants his as*h*le back?

Don't move. I want to forget you just the way you are.

If Moses had met you there would have been an extra commandment.

I bet your gene pool doesn't have a deep end.

That's fascinating. I could listen to you for... seconds.

If I've said anything to insult you, I want you to know, I mean it.

He's nothing, if not a great wit. In which case, he's nothing!

I'll look forward to running into you again. Perhaps on a pedestrian crossing somewhere...

He was going to be circumcised but the surgeon said: 'I can't operate... There's no end to this pr*ck'.

When he was circumcised they threw the wrong bit away. (IF THE PUNTER REPLIES: "I'm not circumcised" THEN SAY... I know you not. I spoke to the surgeon... He said he couldn't do the job because there's no end to this pr*ck).

I could eat a bowl of alphabet soup/spaghetti and sh*t a funnier line than that!

It's clear that this guy is a shining wit... I think I said that right... (whining sh*t)

There's always one pr*ck in every bunch of roses.

Why don't you pull your bottom lip over your head and swallow?

Why don't you pull your foreskin over your head, take a p*ss and drown yourself?

Are they your first teeth? They'll be your last if you don't shut up.

I hope your next sh*t is a hedgehog.

I hope your balls turn square and rot away at the corners.

I bet he never farts. His mouth isn't closed long enough to build up enough pressure.

I bet your wife wishes your d*ck was as big as your mouth.

SMART COMEBACKS FOR OFT-HEARD HECKLES

(YOU'RE CR*P!)   I know! And I'm <u>still</u> earning a living. Just think how much I could have made if I was any good at this!

(YOU'RE CR*P!) Yes, but if you were any better the seats would all be facing you.

(YOU'RE FAT!) I'm not fat. I'm just short for my weight. By my doctor's estimation I should be seventeen foot nine!

(YOU'RE FAT!) Yes, do you know why I'm so fat? Because every time I shag your sister she gives me a great big piece of cake...

(YOU'RE BALD!) I'm not bald; I've just got a wide parting. No hair, just a wide parting.

(TELL US A JOKE!)   OK. An Englishman, an Irishman and a Scotsman walk into a bar... And they all think you're a d*ckhead.

(GET ON WITH IT!) Oh! Somebody's on a promise...   I should take her home mate, I think she's ready. I wouldn't want to be in the way...

(GET OFF!) I get paid for making a tw*t of myself, what's your excuse?

(GET OFF!) You do all the talking you like, there's only me getting paid for it!

(WE'VE HEARD IT!) A bloke takes his dog to the vet. He goes back the next day and the vet says: "I've got some good news and some bad news. The bad news is that we've had to amputate all of the dogs legs, the good news is that we've been able to replace them with four brand new tin legs..." TURN TO THE HECKLER AND SAY: "HAVE YOU HEARD IT?" No?... Well you will if it runs past your window tonight...

(OPPORTUNIST HECKLER) Ah, a hit and run heckler! I've obviously scared him off by talking to him. Shame, he was so gentle in the toilets before the show.

THE CD PUT-DOWN

IF YOU SELL CD'S AND MERCHANDISE, THIS COULD BE VERY USEFUL. I DON'T SELL CD'S BUT I DO USE THIS AS A PUT-DOWN. WHILE YOU'RE DOING YOUR SALES PITCH, SOMEONE WILL PROBABLY SHOUT OUT THAT THEY WON'T BUY ONE. JUST SAY:

"I know <u>you</u> don't want to buy one, you obviously prefer the sound of your own voice".

OR AS A PUT-DOWN...

"I've actually got a CD for sale after the show. Do you want to buy one? No, well of course you don't. You obviously prefer the sound of your own voice".

OR IF THEY SHOUT 'YES':

"You see, if you shut up and listen you could hear it all now and save yourself a fortune".

A MISERABLE FACE

USE THESE WHEN YOU HAVE A MISERABLE FACE IN THE AUDIENCE

Are you enjoying yourself? Yes? Let your face know, will you?

I'd hate to go home to her with a quid (dollar) short in my wages.

I'd hate to send her for the midwife...

How much do you charge to haunt a house?

Where do you come from, Goole? (Ghoul)

Did you smile then or was it just wind?

(TO A MISERABLE FEMALE) Cheer up, you might have got your dates mixed up...

PUT-DOWNS FOR GIRLS

(GROUP) Welcome along girls. Streets quiet tonight, are they?

Did you girls come together? I'd like to have seen that...

Are you two sisters? Left Cinderella at home, did we?

Are you sisters? No? Same hairdresser then, eh?

Thanks, Mum...

(NOISY FEMALE) Do you make this much noise when you're having sex? No? Quick! Somebody shag her!

(THREE FEMALES) Here they are... The three nuns. Never had none, don't want none, never gonna get none.

I may not be your cup-of-tea but at least I haven't got a fat ass. (A CRUEL BUT EFFECTIVE PUT-DOWN FOR A FEMALE LOUDMOUTH – USE ONLY AS A LAST RESORT).

I like your hair. Did you come on a Motorbike?

Who lit the fuse on your Tampax? (Tampon)

(WOMAN WITH YOUNGER BOYFRIEND) You shouldn't shout out like that, you're embarrassing your son.

It's rude to ask a woman her age so... How much do you weigh?

I'm not going to argue with you, I think you're a Babe. Have you seen the movie?

I wouldn't mind being the last man on Earth, just to see if the girls have been telling me the truth all these years...

It must be really hard to die your roots black when you've got blonde hair.

You'd make a good burglar, you ass would rub your footprints out.

You can sit down now, we've seen the outfit.

Wow! Primark's taken a hammering! (USE ANY DISCOUNT CLOTHING STORE)

I don't know why she's being nasty to me now... She was so gentle with me in the car park before the show...

DRINK/DRUNKS

He had all his toes amputated so he could stand nearer the bar.

He spilled his beer so much he's got cirrhosis of the shoelaces.

When he dies they'll have to beat his liver to death with a stick.

Someone threw a petrol bomb in here last week. Before it could go off, she drank it.

He's on a whiskey diet at the moment. He lost 3 days last week.

His mate had a terrible accident... He drowned in a vat of beer. Police are treating it as suspicious... He got out 3 times for a p*ss.

I thought alcoholics were supposed to be anonymous...

Has no-one ever told you, you shouldn't drink on an empty head?

He went to a DIY store last week to buy some paint stripper. They said: 'Do you want a one litre or a two litre'? He said 'give me one out of the fridge...'

What are you drinking? Night nurse?

What are you drinking? Embalming fluid?

What are you drinking? Liquid Kryptonite?

(DRUNK MAN ACTING STUPID) I'll have a pint of what he's just had...

I was like that after my first beer/shandy/sherry.

He drinks like a two headed alcoholic on an all-inclusive holiday

He's mixing vodka and lucozade. He's as p*ssed as a rat, but in the morning he'll be as fit as a fiddle.

I've read so much about the dangers of alcohol that I've given up reading.

One more drink and she'll be under the table. In fact, I think one more drink and she'll be under the landlord.

Here we go, the charge of the light-ale brigade.

I see liquor mortis has set in.

ANNIVERSARY / BIRTHDAY / WEDDING

YOU CAN TAG THESE ON TO ANY BIRTHDAY AND ANNIVERSARY ANNOUNCEMENTS YOU MAKE. THEY MAKE IT LOOK LIKE YOU'RE PERSONALISING A JOKE TO AN OCCASION, USING YOURSELF (AND NOT THE GUESTS) AS THE BUTT OF THE JOKE.

It's our anniversary next week. I've booked a table just for me & the wife. I hope it goes better than last year... She only potted three balls.

I asked my wife what she wanted for her birthday. She said she wanted a divorce. I said: 'I wasn't thinking of spending that much'.

My Grandma died on her 85th birthday. It was very sad... We were only half way through the bumps at the time...

I asked what she wanted for her birthday. She said 'I want you to smother me with diamonds'. I couldn't afford the diamonds so I just smothered her

How come they say 'Always the bridesmaid never the bride'? They don't say the same at funerals do they? 'Always the pall-bearer never the corpse'?

At weddings some old-timer always comes up to me, points at the happy couple and says 'you'll be next...'. I get my own back these days... I say the same to them at funerals.

OPENINGS

There's a lovely warm feeling in here tonight, the last time I had a feeling as warm as this I'd p*ssed myself.

(SMALL VENUE) Good evening and welcome to the Royal Albert Hut / Madison Square Garage.

(SMALL VENUE) – Good evening Wembley!

Thank you for that wonderful sitting ovation.

Did anyone get in tonight without paying? (PULL A TOY CAP GUN AND FIRE IT) Anyone else?

It's always a great pleasure to appear amongst your friends. It's a pity none of them turned up, really.

(AFTER A BOISTEROUS WELCOME) Ah, you don't frighten me I've played (LOCAL ROUGH TOWN).

When I told My friend I was playing here tonight he said "On No!... (BIG PAUSE) They're really posh and upper class there". (SOMEONE ALWAYS REACTS HERE. NOW SAY...) "You weren't in that night."

(AFTER A LOUSY INTRODUCTION) Thank you, Doctor Crippen. (Ted Bundy)

We're celebrating tonight. It's 50 years to the day since the balcony collapsed.

If you've seen me before then you can rest assured that the show tonight is up to the usual sub-standard.

The show tonight is educational. By then end you'll be saying: 'That's taught me a lesson'...

You've heard of the 'March of Time', Ladies and Gentlemen I give you 'The Waste Of Time', here he is...

(OVERWEIGHT) It takes guts to do that... and here's a man who's more than qualified...

(OVERWEIGHT) He's an all round entertainer. Well, he's all round anyway...

(OVERWEIGHT) He's put a bit of weight on since we last saw him. I mentioned it to him and he said: "I know, I've had a lot on my plate recently".

He's one of the finest minds in the country. He's no good in the town, but in the country, he's unbeatable...

SOMETHING BREAKS/BAD LUCK

It's got to go back in the morning...

Ah well, if at first you don't succeed. So much for skydiving...

I've had bad luck like this all my life... I went to a funeral yesterday and caught the wreath...

I woke up this morning to find my water-bed had burst. Then I remembered I haven't got a water bed

I woke up this morning, put on my shirt and the button fell off, opened the car door and the handle fell off... I've been dying for a p*ss all day...

Look at this place... The furniture goes back to Louis the Fourteenth... This goes back to (Asda/Wal Mart) on the fifteenth.

QUICK LAUGHS

I never wanted to be a big star and so far that's worked perfectly to plan...

My memory is so good that I remind the elephants...

Do you fancy a sing-song? (Yes) Off you go then...

Anyone in from the council? Look, sweat! (DAB YOUR FOREHEAD)

Comedy is like sex. The more noise you hear, the better you think you're doing.

I come from a family of criminals. I turned to showbiz because I didn't want to follow in my father's fingerprints.

(LOOK INTO THE WINGS AS IF ARGUING) I don't want to come off...

(PERSON ON STAGE) Your hands are shaking... Shame to waste it... (MAKE AS IF TO PUT PERSON'S HAND IN YOUR POCKET)

I wish I was out there watching this...

A survey has revealed that 95% of men masturbate in the shower. The other 5% sing. Do you know what they sing? I thought not.

MADE UP NAME

OCCASIONALLY WHEN YOU ASK A HECKLER THEIR NAME THEY WILL MAKE UP A FALSE ONE. IT'S USUALLY PRETTY OBVIOUS BECAUSE IT'S OFTEN A SLIGHTLY FUNNY OR UNUSUAL NAME. IF THIS HAPPENS SAY...

(Cuthbert)? That's not your real name is it? What's the matter, has the Doctor told you you've got to live as a woman for a year to prove you're serious about the operation?

(Manuel)? That's not your real name is it? This guy's an undercover heckler! He even heckles under an assumed name!

81

SITUATIONS

PERSON(S) LEAVING

If I'd have known you were leaving I'd have done my ending first.

No, wait, it gets better!

Has your mum come for you?

(FEMALE HALF OF COUPLE LEAVES) Was that your girlfriend? I bet you don't know who she's texting outside now, do you?

(MASS EXODUS - START TO COMMENTATE LIKE A HORSE RACE) The guy in the white jacket is ahead of the field, but is quickly overtaken by the woman in the blue jacket, coming up on the inside is the guy with the red coat...

Ladies and Gentlemen thank you for the walking ovation.

Is this a shortcut to (LOCAL PLACE)?

Is this a shortcut to (LOCAL DISCOUNT STORE – PRIMARK ETC.)?

Here we go, the Jury's retiring...

Is this a sponsored walk?

Was it something I said?

WALKING PAST WITH DRINKS

(HANDS FULL OF DRINKS) Look at this! He's panic buying!

I'll come round your house and walk round while you're performing

Sit down, we've seen the shirt

He's had all his toes amputated so he can stand nearer the bar

Someone threw a petrol bomb through the window last week. Before it could go off, she drank it.

He drinks like a two-headed alcoholic on an all-inclusive holiday.

He's not from round here... He's taken his hand off his glass / put his drink down.

He only drinks to steady his nerves. Last night he got so steady he couldn't move.

LEAVING (FOR TOILETS)

Mention my name, you'll get a good seat!

(WHEN THEY BACK-CHAT ON THE PUT-DOWN) I'll get you on your way back... It'll be the longest p*ss you've ever had!

There he goes,
On his toes,
For a wee-wee I suppose...
He looks a nice and friendly chap,
He might be going for a...

Remember you can only get a sexually transmitted disease off a toilet seat if you sit down before the other fella gets up.

You've heard of a standing ovation... This is a walking ovation.

No wait, it gets better!

The management have asked me to point out that the sign in the toilets that says 'wet paint' is not an instruction...

It must be awful... having to empty a bag halfway through a show...

There he is, off to the toilets again. He uses two hands you know. Mind you, he is p*ssing on six fingers.

Could you hear us in there? No? Well we could hear you out here.

A COUPLE OF QUICK *'LEAVING FOR TOILETS'* SKITS:

1. *WHEN SOMEONE GETS UP AND LEAVES FOR THE TOILETS SAY TO YOUR AUDIENCE...*

    'When he comes back, I'll say "...and the vicar said yes, but not with a cement mixer..."'

    THEN TELL THEM TO LAUGH REALLY LOUD AS IF IT'S THE PUNCHLINE TO A JOKE. WHEN THE PERSON RETURNS WAIT A FEW MINUTES THEN JUST SAY THE LINE. THIS GETS A BIG LAUGH.

2. *WHEN SOMEONE EXITS FOR THE TOILETS, GET THE PERSON HE'S SAT WITH TO SWAP TABLES WITH SOMEONE NEARBY. PLAYS FOR A BIG LAUGH AS THE PERSON COMES BACK, SITS NEXT TO THE WRONG PERSON AND THINKS THEY'VE SAT AT THE WRONG TABLE.*

GOOD AUDIENCE

What a nice audience, I wish I had a better act...

Was that a round of applause or has somebody put the chips (fries) in?

What a nice audience, I suppose I'll have to do the full act now.

(WITH A CORDED MICROPHONE) 'Bless you, bless you...' [THEN HOLD THE MIC UPSIDE DOWN, HANGING BY THE CABLE AND SWING THE MICROPHONE BACK-AND-FORTH LIKE THE POPE GIVING A BLESSING.]

What a nice crowd. Forgive me if I'm looking a little lost, I've never got this far before...

What a lovely audience. I'd invite you back to the hotel for coffee but I've only got one of those little things of milk and two tea bags.

Thank you so much for the warm hand on my entrance.

What a great reception... It's like being on Jerry Springer/Jeremy Kyle

(LOOK BEHIND YOU) I thought someone else had come on...

What a lovely audience. Can I book you for tomorrow night?

They say that a performer is only as good as his audience. Well I'd like to say that I've been brilliant tonight...

EMPTY/DEAD AUDIENCE

It's nice to have so many tables and chairs with us tonight!

If it carries on like this we can share a taxi home

This is a lively table... It sleeps eight.

What are they drinking at the back?   Bostick? / Superglue / Night Nurse / Nytol / Embalming Fluid...

This happened last week. I played a gig and there were only eight people in. The compere said: 'Don't worry there's a bus coming soon'. Half an hour later the bus arrived, they all got on and left.

What a polite audience, you covered your mouth when you yawned...

This is a very exclusive club. Notice how few we let in tonight.

It's like working in Outpatients.

I've seen happier looking Bulldogs.

I've been in bed with more people than this...

I could tell you a joke each and we could be home by 8.30.

You enjoying this? Let your face know, will you?

Let's all join hands and contact the living!

Is this your first time as an audience?

You've been a challenge tonight... and you've won.

Good evening Wembley! (FUNNY IN A SMALL EMPTY VENUE)

Look at all these tables and chairs. It looks like an eviction.

There's a lot of furniture in tonight. It looks like IKEA

This might be a night out for you, it's a career for me!

As you can see, I'm still packing 'em in!

FLUFFED LINES

I'm keeping the teeth and getting rid of the mouth

I must get these teeth fixed...

I'm breaking these teeth in for an elderly neighbour.

I'm breaking these teeth in for the horse/dog.

I'm having trouble rolling my tongue around my R's (arse). You might have experienced something similar...

My speech hasn't been the same since I beat my tongue wafer thin with a meat tenderizer.

I just got the nose fixed now the mouth won't work.

I've always been very careful with my English, but very careless with my Scotch.

LAUGHS (NONE)

You might as well laugh, your money's gone.

I'll keep going till I find one you like.

Hasn't it gone quiet, shall we go somewhere for a drink?

Was it cold in the ground this morning?

Thank you! Both of you...

Thank you. Now that the applause has thoroughly died down...

So this is the place where they send acts to stop them getting big headed...

(TO MISERABLE WOMAN) Cheer up, you might have got your dates mixed up. (FOLLOW UP WITH) Imagine going home to her with a quid short in your wages...

Smile, it's the second best thing you can do with your mouth. Kissing is the best. That is what you were thinking isn't it?

That's my motto... If you can't get a laugh, start a fight!

I know you're out there I can hear you breathing...

Here's another one you won't get...

I don't mind if you don't laugh a lot, just so long as you show willing.

I don't mind if you don't laugh, but could you just smile really loud?

If you hear one you like just put your hand up.

You don't frighten me I've played (NAME OF LOCAL VENUE).

(NAME OF WELL-KNOWN LOCAL PERSON) ...told me that one.

(WALK FROM ONE SIDE OF THE STAGE TO THE OTHER) Comedy over here, tragedy over here...

What makes you laugh, tax returns?

I'll do an easy one...

What makes you laugh, open graves?

You could hear a pin drop...   Not that it bothers me. The hand grenade bothers me.

You'll be driving home tonight and you'll just get it... You'll say "Oh I get it now! I wish I'd laughed while I was there". Or:

You'll wake up tomorrow morning and go: "Oh I get it!   I wish I'd laughed while I was there"

A minutes silence for a joke that just died!

What's the matter, do I owe you money?

You look like you're waiting for the act to show up, this is it!

Repeat the tag line then walk to the opposite side and say it again. Then walk back to the original position.

You'll get it later...

I can hear my hair growing...

Strange, I did a gig at an old folks home last night. When I told that one they p*ssed themselves.   Nobody laughed, they just p*ssed themselves.

There are another 50 like that to come so you'd better start laughing...

LAUGH (STRAY)

I've just jogged her memory...

Are you laughing at something I just said, or something he's just done?

Steady on, someone else has got to sit in that seat.

I haven't heard a laugh like that since my wedding night.

I should take her home pal, I think she's ready...

(Shriek and laugh) Could someone get a basket for those eggs...

Can you explain to everyone else just how funny this really is...

Could you move around a little, my agent's in...

You just got it! (REPEAT PUNCH LINE FROM A JOKE 10 MINUTES AGO – NOT THE ONE YOU JUST DID)

Which one are you laughing at? (REPEAT A TAG LINE FROM EARLIER)

If she faints stick her head between her legs. Make sure she's not smoking a cigarette first.

Unexpected laugh... Check your flies.

APPLAUSE (LAME/NONE)

Thank you for that burst of indifference...

Thank you! Both of you...

Now that the applause has thoroughly died down...

Thank you for that wonderful sitting ovation

The audience last night were so stunned they forgot to applaud too...

There's two ways to do this, one is with applause...

That's what I like... A challenge

Well, you've been a challenge... and it looks like you've won...

Thank you for the applause. It sounds like a head slapping contest.

It sounded like a bus load of nudists sitting down.

This happened last night.. I thought I was getting applause, I looked up and someone was slapping the ketchup out of the bottle.

I can see <u>you</u> like it, but what about everybody else?

Will you just explain to everyone else just how impressive this really is?

Thank you for the clap, I've been trying to avoid it for years...

'Thank you for the clap...' as the Bishop said to the chorus girl.

Ah! The sound of one person clapping. I haven't heard that since my wedding night...

One person clapping. Always a bit embarrassing. Particularly after an orgy.

Thank you. For a moment I thought you were all handcuffed.

Thank you. It feels so nice to get a warm hand on your opening.

So this is the place where they send acts to stop them getting big headed...

Thank you for the silent ovation

GREAT REACTION / APPLAUSE

Please... Don't... Stop... (as the applause subsides) Please, don't stop...

Save it for the end I've got a weak finish.

What a lovely audience. I only wish I had a better act.

I wish I was out there watching this.

What a lovely audience. I wish my agent was in.

What a lovely audience. A reaction like that gives you a lovely warm feeling.. A bit like when you p*ss yourself.

Thank you. It feels so nice to get a warm hand on your opening.

Thank you for that lovely reaction. If I look a bit surprised it's because I've never got this far before...

Thank you for that wonderful round of applause. I thought somebody else had come on stage...

SNEEZE

Sorry, I'm allergic to audiences

Every time I sneeze I get an erection. Don't worry I've started taking something for it... Pepper.

I thought it was flu, but it's snot... (it's not)

I could be getting a cold. I slept with the window open last night and influenza (in-flew-enza)

Oh, spray it again!

I said 'say it' not 'spray it'.

YAWN

(SOMEONE YAWNS AT YOU) It's OK, I'll be done in a minute.

Spot the guy who came to the wrong meeting...

It's like working on a trout farm...

Did you know that a yawn is nature's way of letting a husband open his mouth?

Why is it that when you yawn the person standing next to you starts yawning as well? If all the people in the world stood side-by-side there could be one big Mexican yawn...

What a polite audience, you covered your mouth when you yawned...

COUGH

If you start smoking that cough will go away.

Cough it up! It may be a gold watch!

I smoke 40 a day and I can't cough that good.

I should get that checked out, that's how I started.

Quick! Pass him a cigar, he's dying!

(Rhyme)It wasn't the cough that carried him off. It must be the coffin they carried him off in.

Ladies and Gentlemen welcome to 'The Sound Of Mucus'...

DROP SOMETHING

I'll just put that down there for a minute...

(LOUD CLATTER) Someone's dropped a clanger.

(LOUD CLATTER BACKSTAGE) Mice...

Just trying to make it look difficult...

MESS – CONFETTI ETC. ON STAGE

It looks like Coco the clown exploded.

This is not too bad. I used to work in the Circus and I followed the elephant act.

SOMEONE HANDS YOU A NOTE WHILE YOU'RE ON STAGE

READ IT, THEN SAY... "But I don't want to 'get off'..."

MISTAKE – SEE ALSO 'TEETH'.

Everyone makes a mistake once in a while. Lets face it, that's why some of you are here tonight... And why some of us are here at all.

Just trying to make it look difficult...

I knew this would be a good place for a rehearsal...

As you can see this has taken years of practice and devotion...

But first, a song...

It's actually very difficult to make it look like it's going wrong. I've had to practice for many hours to make It look This realistic.

Well don't I feel the as*h*le now...

Well, if I was any good at this I'd be on TV.

SEE ALSO 'SOMETHING BREAKS/BAD LUCK' ON PAGE 80

SOUND & MICROPHONES

Can you hear me at the back?... (No). Then how do you know what I'm asking?

(Low feedback) God bless this ship and all that sail in her.

(High feedback) ...I think that just loosened my fillings.

They spent thirty thousand pounds/dollars on this event... and 2.99 on the microphone...

Even karaoke nights get mics that work!

I did complain to the management about the acoustics in this theatre. The manager has assured me that they'll order some traps in the morning and get rid of them completely.

(ECHO) It sounds like a staff call in a swimming pool.

(BUMP INTO MICROPHONE) "Sorry, Mike"

I'll move the microphone stand out of the way. That way you'll know I'm the one with the beard (or glasses/moustache/hair etc.)

(OVERWEIGHT) I'll move the mic stand out of the way, otherwise you'll not be able to see me.

(VISUAL GAG) Lift the Mic stand to show the three feet and say: 'Anyone want their passport stamping for the Isle of Mann?

(VISUAL GAG) Lift the microphone out of the stand and put the mic to your ear, then sway the mic stand left and right as if using a mine detector. Then say: 'You can't be too careful'.

Is it too loud for you? I don't mean the microphone, I mean the shirt.

(VISUAL GAG) Lift the mic stand and hold it behind you against your back with the pole extending vertically above you, then say: 'Quick impression... A bumper car' (dodgem) then run around the stage.

LIGHTING / STAGE

LIGHTS FAIL:

Put some lights on... I'm not a moth.

I guess we could wait till the sun comes up.

I bet you anything the <u>outside</u> lights are on...

Anyone got any change for the meter?

That's the last time we buy low voltage bulbs from Ikea

Anyone got any credit on their top-up card?

.

Aren't these the same lights they use to keep the fries warm in McDonald's?

I've just found out that the guy who operates the spotlight has been having an affair with my wife. Flash the light if you kissed her (LIGHT FLASHES), Flash the light if you've put your arms around her (LIGHT FLASHES), flash the light if you made love to her (LIGHT FLASHES). How many times? (ALL THE LIGHTS IN THE THEATRE FLASH LIKE CRAZY)

(ORCHESTRA PIT) – I see they've closed the pits round here too.

(CURTAINS CLOSING) I get nervous up here. The last time I saw curtains close like that we never saw my Granddad again.

(STAMP YOUR FOOT ON THE STAGE) Just checking... My brother once went through a platform like this and broke his neck. If it hadn't been for the rope around his neck he'd have broken both his legs as well...

PERSON TAKES PHOTOGRAPH (FLASH)

That'll be fifty pence (cents) please...

No photographs. For security reasons. Social Security reasons.

You're not from the Inland Revenue, are you?

(OVERWEIGHT) The last person who took my photograph charged for a group shot.

Bang goes my invalidity claim...

I'll buy the negatives!

PERSON WALKS ON STAGE

It's just a stage you're going through...

Are you an actor? (No) Well in that case get your feet off the stage.

MOTHS/FLIES ON STAGE

Did you ever wonder what moths bumped into before they invented light bulbs?

This _must_ be a good act, 1,000 flies can't be wrong.

A moth! That's good news, that means the boss is counting the wages!

No flies on my act! Except this one who obviously missed a meeting...

BURP

I'm glad you brought that up. And your last name...?

That reminds me, I must pay the gas bill

Save the big bits, we'll make soup!

I'm glad you got that off your chest.

Just sounds like a load of hot air to me.

VOMITING

"Save me the green bits!"

I was like that after my first pint...

That's it, get it up, you'll feel a lot better... Anyone else have the scampi?

What you been drinking, liquid kryptonite?

Anyone here ordered a pizza?

Ah, my favourite restaurant... 'Twice seen cuisine'!

FART

Was that a voice from the back?

(BRING OUT A TISSUE/HANDKERCHIEF) You might be needing this...

If I were you I'd wipe my ass and call that a sh*t (A STRONGER VERSION OF THE ABOVE)

I didn't ask what your name was...

Farts are like opinions. We all have them, but we don't necessarily want to share other people's.

That just sounds like a load of hot air to me...

I think you're blowing this out of all proportion...

Speak up, Brown, you're through!

Did the earth move for you?... Your friends will.

I should nip and check that out, it sounded a bit close to the cloth to me...

Did you force that one or did it catch you by surprise?

Are you being rude or just passing an opinion?

No more curried rhubarb for you!

That's a sign of old age... Your dreams get dryer and your farts get wetter.

How are you spelling that...?

You're going to have to lay off the lettuce...

BUTTONS

(FALLS OFF) I wouldn't mind but it's got to go back in the morning.

(FALLS OFF) It's been like this all day... I put my (shirt) on; the button falls off, I pick my suitcase up and the handle falls off... I haven't dare take a p*ss all day!

I asked my mum to sew me a button on my shirt. Look at this... (OPEN YOUR JACKET TO REVEAL A HUGE OVERSIZE BUTTON SEWN RANDOMLY IN THE MIDDLE OF YOUR SHIRT)

LOUD VOICE ABOVE ALL OTHERS

In every bunch of roses there's always one isn't there?

Ah, I can see you're in... Will you be staying long?

My mum's in... (or dad)

There he is, sat next to the wall... That's plastered as well.

Oh, sorry, have we woken you up?

Yes, I knew you wouldn't like it. It's obvious you prefer the sound of your OWN voice

Just because you can grow hair around it doesn't mean you should act like one!

Thanks for joining in. I'll come round your house and shout out while you're performing.

Do you shout out like this when you go to the movies?

Thanks for joining in, mind if I take it from here?

I bet your gob's happy when you're asleep.

PHONE

It's your babysitter. She wants to know where the fire extinguisher is.

If that's for me, tell 'em I'm busy.

Answer that, it might be for me...

If that's (Simon Cowell), tell him I'm on a gig...

That rings a bell...

(FEMALE HALF OF COUPLE LEAVES THE ROOM) Is that your girlfriend? I bet you don't know who's she texting outside, do you?

(PHONE RINGS IN AUDIENCE. TAKE THE PHONE FROM THEM AND ANSWER IT) "Hello"? "He's watching a show at the moment. You're actually on stage now, yes, what's your name?" (GET THE CALLER'S NAME) "Hang on a minute, I'll introduce you to the audience... "Say hello to (Julie) after three... One, two, three... (Audience respond). "What did you want (Julie)"? (Then turn to the phone's owner) "Your shed's on fire, she wants to know if she should phone the fire brigade"?

LATECOMERS

Where are you from? (Place) Well I came all the way from (London) and I got here before you..

It's alright, I was just killing time till you got here, you haven't missed a thing.

What time do you call this? The show started at 7.00. Anyway Ladies and Gentlemen, you've been a lovely audience... Thank you and goodnight!

Welcome along. Have a seat. You're just in time for the collection.

Must be a (Skoda) driver. He set off at six but had to push it the rest of the way. (ANY CAR HERE)

Welcome along. You've not missed much. We've all just stood up and introduced ourselves individually, so... *(THEN THRUST THE MICROPHONE AT THEM)*

FLATTERING REMARKS – Responses to

Oh, you're only saying that because it's true.

I always said that you had impeccable taste...

You know, I don't care what everyone else says about you... I think you're all right.

NO REACTION / SLOW REACTION TO QUESTION

You can talk to me I'm not on DVD

Look who I've asked... It's Forrest Gump

(UNINTELLIGIBLE REPLY) Is it a film, a book or a play?

(UNINTELLIGIBLE REPLY) All the words are there, you've just got to get them in the right order...

Look at all the people in here and I had to go and ask the village idiot.

Is the question too difficult?

We'll start with a few easy ones first, what's your name?

Parlez Vous Anglais? Speak-o De English?

This'll be out on DVD before we get this sorted...

Do you want to start with a few questions on sport and warm up gradually?

You can answer me if you like, I'm not asking you for a kidney here...

You're looking at me as if you're waiting for the act to show up. This is it!

What's this, a staring contest?

I know you're out there I can hear you breathing.

Am I facing the right way?

NOISE

I'm sorry, I didn't bring microphones for everyone...

Sorry, was I talking when you were? How rude of me.

I think they're training me to be a police horse.

Can you hear me at the back... (No). Then how do you know what I'm asking?

Can you hear me up the back? (Yes)   Do you like it up the back?

(Noisy female) Do you make this much noise when you're having sex? No? Quick! Somebody shag her!

(loud noise backstage) Someone's dropped a clanger

(loud noise backstage) Mice...

Can I get a little bit of quiet here? Let's pretend the act's on.

Ssssh. Pretend it's bingo.

(WAIT A MOMENT THEN SAY REALLY LOUD)... "Sex!" (IT WILL GO QUIET HERE, THEN SAY)   ...Now that I've got your attention...

MOVEMENT/FIDGETING

(WALKING ABOUT) Is this a sponsored walk?

(WALKING ABOUT) Is this a short cut to (name of local town)?

(WALKING ABOUT) Is this a short cut to (local discount clothing store)?

What are you fidgeting for, has your ass gone to sleep? I thought so, I just heard it snore.

Don't pick your nose mate, we've just swept up...

(ITCHING/SCRATCHING) He went out with a girl last night who had everything. Now it looks as if he's got it too...

What's this, a walking ovation?

(WALKING GROUP) I'm looking for Snow White and the other three...

(WALKING OUT) Look at this, the Jury's retiring...

(WALKING OUT) Where are you going, is there a collection?

(WALKING PAST WITH A PRONOUNCED LIMP) I see you're still taking it up the ass...

EXPLETIVES – SHOUTED OUT

YOU CAN USE THESE AS SNAPPY ANSWERS WHEN SOMEONE SHOUTS SWEAR WORDS AT YOU FROM THE AUDIENCE:

"F*ck Off"   *I'm sorry, I don't do requests.*

"B*llocks"   *I didn't ask you what keeps your ears apart.*

"Kiss My Ass"   *No problem. Do you have a map? You'd make a good burglar, your ass would rub your footprints out.*

PHYSICAL APPEARANCE

HAIR / HEAD

I bet your forehead can keep the rain off your shoes...

Put your hat on there's a Woodpecker flying about

I've seen more hair in soup

Who parted your hair, Moses?

Look at that, he's spent all day doing his hair and come out without it.

If his hair gets any further back he'll be combing his ass.

Are you two sisters? No? Same hairdresser then, eh?

Who cut your hair, the council?

They've just invented a new shampoo for him. It's called Go-and-Wash

I like your hair. Did you come on a motorbike?

She's got her hair in a bun... and her nose in an egg sandwich

It must take you ages to dye your roots black...

(Frizzy hair) BLOW ON THE HAIR AND SAY: "One o' clock" (blow again) "Two o' clock" (blow again)... (AS KIDS DO WITH DANDELION FLOWERS)

(Frizzy hair) BLOW INTO THE HAIR AS IF BLOWING INTO A MICROPHONE AND SAY: "One-two, one, two".

Just because you can grow hair round it doesn't mean that you should talk like one...

(Mohican) Thank your lucky stars that you don't have ginger hair, otherwise that would look like a giant fish finger on your head.

HAIR - BALD

(Bald patch) I should take that wig back, it's got a hole in it.

He's got a wide parting. No hair, just a wide parting

He uses 'wash-and-go' shampoo. He's washed it and it's gone

He's not really bald, he's just got a tall face

Bald at the front means your a great thinker, bald at the back and you're a great lover. Bald all over: You just think you're a great lover.

Lean forward, your head's dazzling me!

He looks like a boiled egg that's been dropped on the carpet

Are you bald or is your neck blowing bubble gum?

If your hair gets any further back you'll end up combing your ass

Who parted your hair.... Moses?

I've seen more hair in soup

My hair is going a little thin but then again who wants fat hair?

(Bald heckler) Crikey! I'm being heckled by a Genie.

I'm not actually bald, I'm just taller than my hair.

(TO A BALD GUY) I bet you feel like an egg in the morning.

FACIAL HAIR - MOUSTACHE

Is that a moustache or are you eating a shredded wheat?

She's got everything a man could want... Muscles, moustache...

He's only grown a moustache so he could look like his mother

His nose is so important he's underlined it

FACIAL HAIR - BEARD

With that cigarette hanging out of your mouth you look like a sheepdog having a sh*t...

That's a great beard. Let me feel it. I'm not gay it's just that there wasn't any paper in the gents toilets.

Look at that, shaves his head, grows a beard. I bet you have a laugh in the hall of mirrors. I bet you look normal.

Oh look, he's growing his own tobacco...

A goatee! Got down to it one night and came away with it, eh?

(BEARD AND BALD) Looks like he's got his head on upside-down.

(WHITE BEARD) ...and my lad wants a bike next Christmas, not a colouring book and crayons like you brought last year!

You look like a rat peering through a bog brush.

FACIAL HAIR – SIDEBURNS

Are they sideburns or are you on the phone?

Ladies and Gentleman, Elvis is in the building...

That's the kind of facial hair you only see on shortbread tins.

Look at the sideburns! It looks like you're between two lamb chops.

Ginger sideburns – It looks like you've got two fish fingers stuck to your face.

UGLY

How much do you charge to haunt a house?

That face could frighten a police horse / police dog.

She's got a face that could stop a bus.

His face could stop a clock.

Are you two sisters? What happened, you left Cinderella at home?

Ugly? I bet if a cannibal saw you he'd order a salad.

Last time I saw a face like that was in the thirteenth round.

If I had a face like yours I'd stand on a wall and throw a brick at it. On second thoughts you'd better stand on a brick and throw a wall at it.

I bet you have to sneak up on the mirror.

I bet when you suck a lemon, the lemon pulls a face.

I've seen ugly before, but you abuse the privilege.

I won't take the p*ss. Nature did that already.

You have to be over 18 to look at her.

It looks like he fell out of the ugly tree and hit every branch on the way down.

I bet your pram had shutters on it.

I bet your dummy had a twelve inch flange.

I bet when you were born the Midwife slapped your father.

What's he going to do when his looks fade?

I bet they had to tie a pork chop around your neck so the dog would play with you...

When he was born they knew he was going to be a comedian. The midwife turned to his father and said, "is this a joke"?

I bet they put your picture over the hearth to keep the kids away from the fire.

If you look up 'ugly' in the dictionary, you'll find his photograph.

Are you on your way to a Halloween party?

She went to the North Pole and a seal clubbed her.

Remember... Good looks are only a light switch away.

If beauty's skin deep, she's an onion.

If beauty's skin deep, she's inside out.

A face like a plumbers tool bag.

A face like a blistered p*ss pot.

A face like a bulldog licking puke off a cactus.

A face like a roofer's nail bag.

I bet she has to get the vibrator p*ssed...

If you get laid in here tonight there's a chance for all of us!

What does he do when he wants to pull a face?

He went to see 'The Elephant Man' and spent half the night signing autographs...

WRINKLES

You've got enough wrinkles to hold 3 days of rainfall

She burned her bra. With the breasts hanging it took all the lines out of her face.

His head has so many wrinkles that his hat has a left hand thread

It's like looking over the top of a sliced loaf

Are those stretch marks round your mouth?

She stood naked in front of her husband and said "what do you think"? He said "It wants ironing".

TEETH

I bet you could eat an apple through a tennis racket

I've seen better teeth on a pumpkin

Teeth like Sugar Puffs

Teeth like Tombstones

Teeth like a Witch Doctor's necklace

Teeth like playing cards

Teeth like a Grand National winner (Kentucky Derby)

Teeth like poker dice

(one tooth) I bet you could chew a polo mint (lifesaver) without breaking it.

(one tooth) He once chewed a polo mint (lifesaver) for an hour and a half. There wasn't a mark on it. OR...

(one tooth) She bit into a dough nut. There wasn't a mark on it

(one tooth) She's Spanish. She's called Juanita (one-eater)

(one tooth) For you it is just a 'tooth' brush isn't it?

The dressing room is so small you can hardly turn around. Good job I didn't bring a tooth brush. (MIME BRUSHING TEETH IN A TIGHT SPACE)

He went to the dentist... He said: 'Can you recommend anything for yellow teeth'? The dentist said 'yes, how about a brown tie'?

EYES

Her eyes are a sort of greeny-blue. I prefer the blue one

She had eyes that were jealous of one-another

Blue eyes – One blew this way one blew the other way

She's got pedestrian eyes. They look both ways

NOSE

Don't pick your nose, we've just swept up

(Big nose) I bet you could smoke a cigar in the shower

(Big nose) If you took cocaine you could inhale Columbia

I bet your nose has got its own postcode

They say 'you can't see past the end of your nose', but in your case that's quite a distance...

You'll never grow a moustache. They don't grow in the shade.

You've got the ugliest nose I've ever seen... And it suits you.

BUST

I used to love big breasts. Till I grew some...

What the Lord has forgotten she's filled up with cotton.

(Big bust) I'm on the peanut and melon diet at the moment. The peanuts aren't working...

It's one of those Tupperware bras. It doesn't do much for your figure but it'll keep what you've got fresh.

It's one of those sheepdog bras... Rounds 'em up and keeps em together.

She doesn't have much to show off. It looks like two aspirins on an ironing board.

I found out how to get a bigger bust without surgery. Get a piece of toilet roll and rub it between your cleavage, it'll give you a bigger bust. Well, it worked on your ass didn't it?

Ass

You'd make a good burglar. Your ass would wipe your footprints out.

She had that much cellulite on her ass she looked like a leather Chesterfield couch.

You're not fat, you're just big-boned. Your ass bone's a hell of a size!

I may not be your cup-of-tea but at least I haven't got a fat ass.
(CUTTING BUT EFFECTIVE PUT-DOWN FOR A 'BIG-BONED' HECKLER)

That ass is so big I bet it's got its own postcode.

You know how to get a bigger bust without surgery? Get a piece of toilet roll and rub it between your cleavage, it'll give you a bigger bust. Well, it worked on your ass didn't it?

THIN

If she had three belly buttons she'd be a flute.

If they put Doc Martens on her she'd look like a golf club.

Does Popeye know you're out tonight?

I've seen more meat on a butcher's apron.

I've seen more meat on a Jockey's whip.

With her fur coat on I bet she looks like a pipe cleaner.

When she drinks tomato Juice I bet she looks like a thermometer.

If she closed one eye I bet she'd look like a needle.

When you lay on the couch I bet you look like a xylophone.

FAT

He said 'You've put some weight on...' I said: 'I know, I've had a lot on my plate recently...'

I bet his passport photograph was taken by satellite.

I bet he was christened at the Sea life Centre.

He's so fat he has to put his belt on with a boomerang.

Her belly is so big it's got its own postcode.

His idea of a balanced diet is a pie in each hand.

He's got a great six-pack. Unfortunately he's drunk five of them.

He's so fat it takes him two trips in a revolving door. OR 'it takes him two trips in a taxi'.

If he climbs on top of you in the night, you'll go through the mattress like chips (French fries).

I bet you've flattened some grass in your time...

You're not fat, you're just big-boned. Your belly bone's particularly impressive...

He doesn't know why he's so fat, he eats each of the four major food groups every day: McDonald's, Pizza Hut, Burger King and Kentucky Fried Chicken... and a diet coke.

I'm just getting into shape for the season. It just so happens that this seasons shape is a sack of horse sh*t...

I'm not fat, I'm just short for my weight. My doctor reckons my ideal height should be sixteen foot nine.

He went to a tailor's. He said 'have you got anything to fit me off-the-peg'? The bloke said 'yes, how about this tie'?

He went to the tailor's. He said have you got anything to fit me off-the-peg? The tailor said 'If we have, somebody's getting the sack'.

He went in a car showroom and said "I want something that will go from nought to a hundred in two seconds flat". They gave him some bathroom scales.

Last birthday, he ate the cake so fast they had to prize his mouth open to blow the candles out.

When he eats he has two glasses of water... One to drink and one to cool his fork down.

When he was at school they asked: "What's your favourite instrument"? He said: "The dinner bell".

If you get laid in here tonight, there's chance for all of us...

It's no use looking for a girlfriend, you can't even get in your own pants.

Always remember that inside every fat person is a thin person screaming to get out... But you can usually shut the b*stard up with biscuits (cookies).

She's got an hourglass figure. Unfortunately most of the sand is at the bottom.

DOUBLE CHIN

(Name a fat celebrity) He's just been on the TV. Apparently he's just announced the opening of another chin.

He's got more chins than Chinatown.

More chins than the Chinese phone book.

It looks like he's peeping though a stack of bagels OR...

'looks like he's leaning on a stack of crumpets'.

There are two things I like about you... Your chin

SHORT

He's so short he has turn-ups on his boxer shorts.

You'd make a good fridge magnet.

Where are Snow White and the other six?

Is he in a trench?

I bet he fell off a key-ring.

I bet he's got a full length photo on his passport.

How far away is he?

Hi Hooooooo.... (SUNG IN THE STYLE OF DISNEY'S 7 DWARFS)

He was worried about what to wear tonight. He's spent half the afternoon pacing up and down _under_ the bed...

I bet he still gets on the bus for half fare.

We don't know where he came from, we just opened the Sugar Puffs one day and there he was! (ANY BREAKFAST CEREAL)

He's living proof that Snow White and Dopey _did_ have sex.

TALL

I bet he has to stand on a chair to brush his teeth.

You're tall. What happened did you fall asleep in a greenhouse?

I bet you grew up when meat was cheap.

I used to go out with a tall girl, but I had to jack it in...

I bet if you drink tomato juice you'd look like a thermometer.

If you put a woolly hat on you'd look like a cotton bud.

If you had three belly buttons you'd be a flute.

He looks a big lad. If you came home and found him in bed with your wife you'd just tuck him in, wouldn't you...

He's a big lad. If he says it's Sunday we'll all start singing hymns...

GLASSES

Look at the glasses! I bet they weren't made in an hour...

His glasses are so thick I bet he can wave at spacemen when he's wearing them.

Look at the size of the glasses. You should have a 'Neighbourhood Watch' sticker in the corner.

If there's any bright sunshine you'll set fire to your eyebrows.

I'd like to mention our special guest... Ladies and Gentlemen it's the Milky Bar Kid!

PUT DOWNS FOR 'PRO' HECKLERS

He only got into showbusiness so he could wear make-up

He's a brilliant entertainer, you ask him...

He's one of the finest talents in the country... Useless in town, but in the country, he's the best!

The Times once described him as: 'A thinking man's continued on page twenty seven'.

There are two things I like about this guy... His face.

Last year my friend said: "I'm leaving. I'm going to go to Las Vegas and I'm gonna make it big. The chances are you'll never see me again..." He said: "I hate this place, I'm off and I'll only ever come back if I fail. Anyway, it's lovely to have him with us tonight..."

CLOTHING & ATTIRE

SUIT/OUTFIT

Sit up straight, pretend the suits fits you.

Nice to see you again. I haven't seen him in years. I can't remember his name but I never forget a suit.

Was that expensive? How much?! You could get a new one for that!

Lovely suit... Great places, aren't they... Charity shops

Bloody hell, Primark's taken a hammering hasn't it? (ANY DISCOUNT STORE)

I bought this suit from a shop that sells slight seconds. You can hardly tell... except that one sleeve is slightly longer than the other two.

This suit is a cross between Versace and Armani: Vermin

The label says 'Armani... and Navy'

It's from a new store. It's a cross between Marks and Spencer and Poundstretcher. It's called Stretchmarks.

I've seen better cloth round cheese.

Look at the suit! There must be a Ford Cortina outside with the seat covers missing...

Nice to see you dressing up for the event... Evening suit... and trainers.

I see your school uniform still fits you.

Nice to see you've come out in your gardening clothes...

The bins are round the back, mate..

If you smartened yourself up you'd make a good tramp .

TIE

What's blue and hangs off a d*ck? His tie!

(SUIT WITHOUT A TIE) I can see you're saving up for a tie to go with that suit.

(SUIT WITHOUT A TIE) Do you make good money? Then you should buy a tie you tight b*stard!

I couldn't get into a club because I wasn't wearing a tie. I went back to my car and put the jump-leads round my neck. The doorman said 'You can come in, but don't start anything...'

I can tell that shirt's Italian. It's got spaghetti down the front.

Look at the tie... Silk from Italy... and ketchup from Burger King.

SHIRT

It's not too loud for you is it?   I don't mean the microphone, I mean the shirt...

I see your school shirt still fits you...

(CHECKED SHIRT) – I've got three-across but I can do f*ck-all with thirteen down. (CROSSWORD PUZZLE)

(LOUD SHIRT) I hear you can get those in bright colours too...

(LOUD SHIRT) Does that shirt have a volume control?

I've seen better cloth round cheese...

Like the shirt? Silk from China... (LOOK CLOSER) ...and gravy from the KFC

(PATTERNED SHIRT) Look at the shirt! You look like a hanging basket.

STRIPES

I should keep moving if I were you, someone might think you're a deck chair and sit on you

What a dress... It looks like a punch and judy booth

(Striped jumper) I thought it was a burglar creeping up on me

It looks like you sat down on 'wet paint'

DRESS

That's a nice dress you're almost wearing.

It's a bingo dress... Eyes down, look in.

It's not so much a dress, more a sort of gown-less evening strap.

Did you make that dress yourself? You did well without a pattern.

Is that chiffon or sh*t on?

What a lovely dress, tell me, is that an upholstery fabric?

You can sit down, we've all seen the dress.

That's a lovely floral print fabric. You look like a hanging basket.

They said it 'looks better on'... To be honest I think it would look better on fire.

It's not so much a dress... By the size of it, it's more like a beer tent.

It's made of latex, lurex and du... ring the night...

EARRINGS/PIERCINGS

There are only two kinds of people that wear earrings. Rent boys and Pirates... and I didn't see a Galleon out on the car park...

When I was a teenager if you got a metal spike through your face they sent you to hospital. Now they send you to University.

My gran had her nipple pierced... She had to take it out, she kept catching her big toe in it.

She had one of those nipple rings... Size of it, it could have been an onion ring.

SHOES

You know what they say about big shoes... Big feet.

You know what they say about men with big shoes... Mine are a bit cramped in these size elevens...

I bought some tortoise skin shoes... It took me three hours to walk out of the shop.

Do you like the shoes? I found them outside a Mosque.

Do you like the shoes? I got them outside a bouncy castle.

(BIG SHOES) Like the shoes? They're Calvin Clown (Klein)

PERSONAL QUALITIES

LAZY/IDLE

He's so lazy he was off work for three weeks with a broken thermos flask

He'll never get hemorrhoids. He's never off his ass long enough.

He's so lazy he's got suntanned armpits

He's so lazy he married a pregnant woman.

He wanted to be a lollipop (school crossing) man. Because they don't start work till they're sixty five

He applied to be a bin man (garbage collector). He thought they only worked on Tuesdays

BORING

You'd make a statue yawn.

If I had 7 days to live I'd marry you. You'd make every day seem like a lifetime.

STUPID

'There are more brains in a pork pie' or 'more brains in a Ginster's pasty'.

They say that blood is thicker than water. He's thicker than both.

He has to take his d*ck out to count to eleven.

He thinks the London Underground is a political party.

I bet his gene pool doesn't have a deep end.

He went for a pizza. The man asked: 'Shall I cut it into four or six'? He said: 'Cut it into four, we'll never eat six'.

There was a power cut while he was out shopping. He stayed on the escalator for hours. I said 'Why didn't you just walk down?'. He said: 'I was on my way up'.

He thought that safe sex was a padded headboard.

If his brains were dynamite he wouldn't have enough to blow his nose.

The mafia will never shoot him for knowing too much...

He tried to commit suicide by throwing himself down the 'up' escalator. It took him 3 and a half hours to fall down the stairs.

DRINKER

See Page 77

MISERLY

He only breathes in.

He wouldn't give a door a bang.

They say that copper wire was invented when he started arguing over a penny.

He came in from work and said to his wife: ' I'm going out, put your coat on'. She says: 'Am I coming with you?'. He said: 'No, I'm turning the central heating off'.

I want to go to Downing Street (The White House)... If only to be nearer my money...

He's the only man I know who's suffering from an in-growing wallet.

PLASTIC SURGERY

I've got a mate who is a plastic surgeon. He's raised a few eyebrows.

The basic rule of thumb with plastic surgery is 'Stop when you look permanently frightened.

She's had so many face-lifts she's got a goatee.

BIG HEAD/VANITY/EGO

He's a genius. I know that because he told me so.

When he has an orgasm he shouts out his own name.

We wears mirrored sunglasses. Unfortunately the mirrors are on the inside.

The good thing about big heads is that they don't talk about other people.

PERFUME

You smell nice. Have you been jogging?

It's a new fragrance. It's called 'Come To Me' and to be honest, it smells like come to me as well.

It's called Canal Number Four'. When you smell it you shout: 'FOUR CANAL!'

That's a lovely perfume you're wearing, what is it? Embalming fluid?

It's that new aftershave, it drives women wild... It smells like money.

They say that genius is 1% inspiration 99% perspiration. You smell like a genius to me...

NAMES

SILLY GAGS FOR USE WHEN ASKING NAMES

Julie   I'm Julie (Duly) impressed

William   William marry me (will ya marry me)

Lorraine   Lorraine in Spain... etc.

Dawn   Dawn go breaking my heart (Don't Go Breaking
                 My Heart - sung)

Sam   Sam enchanted evening (Some enchanted
                 evening - sung)

Wendy   Wen-dy red red robin goes bob bob bobbing...
                 (sung)

Deirdre   I can see Deirdre now Lorraine has gone
                 (Sung as per the song: I Can See Clearly Now..)

Gordon   Gay? (The Gay Gordon is a popular dance)

Mandy   Bank Holiday Mandy?

Jenny   I Jenny (generally) like to ask...

Neil   Kneel on the floor and ask again "what's
                 your name?"

Bob   Bend at the knees in a bobbing fashion then
                 ask again "what's your name"

Simon   Simple, eh?

Matt   Finnish? Ha! (realising) Matt Finish...

Matt   Were you sat by the door, matt?

Sue	You might, after you see what's going to happen.
Veronica	I'll call you Vera and we'll leave the knickers off.
Marge	Don't worry I'll not spread it around.
Jane	Ah, you must be Tarzan... (shake hands with the nearest man)
Pete	Isn't that a posh name for manure?
Owen	(singing) Owen d' saints, go marchin' in...
Stanley	We've got one of your knives.
Alan	We've got one of your keys...
Robin	Banks?
Cliff	You're not from Dover are you?
Jim	You look the sporty type...
Dot	I think I saw you on the horizon.
June	... Busting out all over
Phillip	Oh, I've got one of your screwdrivers
Adam	We've not met before have we? You see, I wouldn't know him from... Well, you get the idea...

WHERE ARE YOU FROM?

Where are you from? (Place)...I'm sorry? (repeat place) Yeah, I heard you I'm just sorry...

That's where they separate the men from the boys. With tyre levers.

The Archbishop of Canterbury has written a letter to all the ladies in... (place) who have been faithful to their husbands. Do you know what it says? No? Ah, well there you go.

PLACES

Anyone in from (local rough town)? Six? Great, enough for a fight!

When you go to...(local town)...there's a sign on the way in. It says 'Welcome to...(place)... Please put your watch back 200 years.

I like it in (local town). I like it anywhere but you can get it in (local town).

I've just come back from (place). Which is the only thing you can do if you're ever lucky enough to find yourself in (place)

It's a lovely place. I was in (place) town centre, somebody shouted 'Stop Thief' and everybody scarpered.

I go there twice a year... To visit my alloy wheels.

Where are you from? (ROUGH PLACE) Leave the silver Audi on the car park won't you?

That's where they separate the men from the boys... With tyre levers.

Where do you come from? (local town) Did you know that the Archbishop of Canterbury has written a letter to all the women in (name of town) that have been faithful to their husbands. Do you know what it says? No? Ah, well there you go...

There are two things that come from (place)... Beautiful women and rugby players... (look at woman in the audience) What position do you play?

There's a great sign on the way in. It says: (town) welcomes careful drivers. The (town) District General Hospital welcomes all the others...

I come from (place). Because of the football team, most people now refer to it as (place) nil.

Even the pigeons fly upside down because there's nothing worth sh*tting on.

It got bombed during the war and they did about 80 quid's (dollars) worth of damage...

What a place that is... 10,000 inhabitants, 2 surnames.

Where are you from? (They reply) Oh that's nice, lovely... (Under your breath) What a sh*t hole that is...

I went to America. They said: "Where do you come from"? I said: "(place)". They said: "What state's that in"? I said: "A bloody hell of a state".

It's a rough place. Mike Tyson was our Avon lady.

They made their own version of Star Wars in (place). It ends with the line: 'Luke... I am your Father... and your Uncle.

I met a bloke from (place). He said I'd like you to meet my wife and sister... There was just one person standing there.

It's a great town. Not twinned with anywhere, instead it's got a suicide pact with Iraq.

They'll never catch anyone for murder in (place). No dental records.

They were going to do a Nativity play in (place) but they couldn't find three wise men and a virgin.

After A Bad Introduction...

Thank you Doctor Crippen (Ted Bundy)...

Thank you for the wonderful introduction. Remind me to come round where you're working tomorrow and knock the bin off your back...

I've heard better announcements on aircraft.

Thank you for that wonderful introduction... Now even I can't wait to hear what I'm going to say!

Thank you for that amazing build-up. Maybe next time you should try to curb your enthusiasm a little?

Now if the Addams Family did introductions...

There's nothing like a big build up... and that was nothing like a big build up.

The Dressing Room

What a lovely dressing room... Well, nail, they've given me.

I have to say that's the most spacious *dressing cupboard* I've ever been in...

It's a good job I didn't bring a toothbrush, there isn't room to turn it around.

The dressing room is so small I put the key in the lock and broke the window.

The dressing room is so cold I opened the wardrobe and my shirt had put my overcoat on.

Event Staff

Our head barman has tonight announced that his girlfriend is expecting twins! When his wife finds out she'll kill him.

We have a special offer on tonight... For tonight only, for every round you buy, the bar staff will give you the correct change!

Look at the bar staff. All keeping busy. The social security inspectors were in here last night. I looked around, there wasn't a soul behind the bar... (MIME AS IF HIDING)

The bar staff are great in here. They put that much water in the beer there's a rainbow over the cellar.

I got pulled by the police last night. He said: 'How much have you had to drink?' I said 'twelve pints'. He said 'Twelve pints! Where have you been?' I said '(name of venue)'. He said 'Oh get on your way, you'll be alright...'

All our doormen tonight are SAS. Soft As Sh*t

What a lovely meal tonight... Our caterers can be contacted via their website: "W-W-W dot E dot Coli forward-slash C.J.D."

Are You Any Good?

AT SOME POINT SOMEBODY IS GOING TO ASK YOU THIS QUESTION. IT USUALLY HAPPENS ON YOUR ARRIVAL AT A VENUE WHEN, IN THE ABSENCE OF ANYTHING INTERESTING TO SAY, SOMEONE WILL ASK YOU 'ARE YOU ANY GOOD'? OR THEY MIGHT INSTEAD SAY SOMETHING LIKE... 'YOU'D BETTER BE GOOD'. WHEN THEY SAY THIS, SIMPLY REPLY...

"If I was any good, I wouldn't be here..."

EXTREME MEASURES

WHAT TO DO WHEN IT
REALLY GOES WRONG

EXTREME MEASURES

This section is all about what to do when the most extreme things happen. This may all sound a bit excessive but these things can and do happen. I give the advice only because I've had to deal with them myself over the years and it can be difficult to know how best to react when you don't have any thinking time.

Thankfully most of these eventualities are rare and the stage is usually a safe place to be. A couple of times I have had things thrown on stage – either from careless drunks, or someone spoiling for a fight – but that's in over 20 years of doing it... And in some very tough venues. Most of your interaction with your audience will be friendly and your interruptions will be limited to the occasional heckler and a dropped tray of drinks.

In terms of the more extreme stuff that can interrupt your show, it is all fairly straightforward to deal with. Remember that in circumstances like these the old adage of 'The show must go on' can go to the wall. In fact it can be more dangerous and pretty foolhardy to carry on.

We will also discuss the subject of 'dying' on stage. It is something that can and most probably will happen to all performers at some point. Knowing how it happens, why it happens and what to do when it does happen will have you one step ahead of the game at all times.

Let's look at some nightmare situations...

A MINUTES SILENCE

This is a subject that has become the subject of showbiz legend and there are many stories of entertainers taking to the stage following 'a minutes silence' for a deceased person. Many of these stories are apocryphal – they lack any real truth – But this has happened to me for real on three or four occasions and there is a further variation on the same theme which has happened a couple of times too.

The first time this happened I was completely floored, I had no idea how to handle it. On one occasion three people from the same venue had died in the same week – I wasn't about to become the fourth.

I was given some advice by a very well established old pro and it has stood me in good stead ever since. It is that advice which I shall relate to you and I can vouch for its efficacy...

The usual scenario goes like this... Someone influential to a venue or organisation has died recently. Prior to the evening's entertainment they decide to hold a minutes silence as a mark of respect for the deceased and then, without a moment's hesitation, look to the stage and say something like: *"And now to make you all laugh, here's James Brandon..."* . Or words to that effect.

It's a nightmare scenario. The advice I have followed for many years concerns the following speech. You simply walk on stage and say the following, inserting the name of the deceased where necessary...

"Ladies and Gentlemen I never knew (Jimmy Scroggins) but I know he was influential to all of you... And if he assembled a group of people like this together in one place then he must have been one hell of a guy. So tonight I'm not doing this show for me and I'm not doing this show for you, tonight, I'm doing this show for (Jimmy Scroggins)..."

Then just get on with your show as normal. Despite it's apparently 'cheesy' sounding delivery, it is another bit of advice that has served me well over the years. It really does work.

The variation on this, is when an introduction destroys your entrance, but in a slightly different way... I once took a last minute cancellation job near Wakefield where the booked act was unable to appear. The agent gave me the address of the venue but failed to inform them of the change of act. I arrived at the venue and the management were annoyed at the change of artist, having not been informed by the agent. Still, I got myself ready and prepared to go on stage. The compere then said:

"Ladies and Gentlemen we have another change of artist again tonight (groans from the audience)... The agent has let us down again. We're getting fed up with this so we've decided that on Monday morning we're giving him the sack and getting a new agent 'cos of the bloody rubbish they've been sending us... And now to entertain you here is James Brandon..." True story.

Where do you go from there? The answer is you can only come back from this one with a big personality and a strong act. Make sure that if this ever happens to you that you 'go up a gear' and give them the best show you're capable of delivering. It is the *only* way out of this situation. If you under-perform you will lose, hands down.

MEDICAL EMERGENCY

You don't need me to tell you that medical emergencies are a serious matter. Depending on what kind of act you perform: Whether you're a singer, comedian or speciality act will depend on how quickly you can stop your act and let the relevant people know what's happening. In serious cases you will need to stop any noise, music or speech and raise the alarm in a calm and professional manner. Don't use the microphone to explain to the rest of the audience what you're doing, just do it. Others may need silence to make an emergency call.

In some cases you may have a better view of what is happening than most other people in the room. If you spot that something is amiss and become aware that someone needs urgent medical attention, just stop what you're doing, get the lights on in the room and exit the stage to call an appropriate person for help.

If required, assist in keeping people calm. You may also be asked to make short public address announcements to ask people to clear the room or whatever. Don't argue, just do what you can to help and use your status among the audience to get them to do whatever is needed to assist in the emergency.

Your first priority is to let a responsible person know that something is wrong and to call the emergency services. The responsible person should inform an appropriately trained 'First Aid' practitioner if necessary. The most important thing from a performance point of view is that if you become aware that there is a *serious* problem in the room, the performance stops until the emergency services have sorted the issue.

There will be some situations where medical treatment is required but it is not necessary to stop the show. You will usually only become aware of these situations when medical professionals actually enter the room.

They are usually able to sort the problem without disrupting the show. Often the person will be removed into the foyer and treated there. If you see this happening, keep a very keen eye on them and check to see if the medical staff indicate that there is a serious problem that would require you to stop the show. If they do motion you to stop, follow their instructions. Medical professionals are vastly experienced in how to handle such matters appropriately. Always follow their instructions.

FIRE ALARMS AND EVACUATIONS

Fire alarms, smoke alarms and other interruptions can bring an abrupt end to your performance. It is important that you do not attempt to crack any jokes in emergency situations. In any case fire alarms will often cut the power to silence any PA equipment and allow the audience to hear the emergency.

Every venue has clear evacuation instructions and fire procedure which you should follow in the event of an emergency. Each venue will also have designated individuals who are tasked with certain roles in the event of an alarm being triggered. Make sure that you familiarise yourself with the fire alarm procedure at any venue that you perform in and follow any instructions given to you as you leave the building.

If you are the person who set the fire alarm off you will can expect a b*llocking at this point.   If you're using smoke and fire effects check the situation first to make sure this doesn't happen to you.

The other situation that I have encountered like this was when someone discharged a dry powder fire extinguisher during a show. The room was very slowly consumed by a white dust cloud like a slow rolling fog and the room had to be evacuated.   It was a weird sight.

Once the dust had settled the audience were let back into the venue and the show continued. Looking back, it seems entirely bizarre (and worthy of note) that the entire audience took their drinks with them to the fire assembly point outside. The comics had a field day with the subject for the remainder of the evening but no jokes were made during the evacuation.

FIGHTS & VIOLENCE

Like I've said many times, the real extreme stuff is rare. Fights are rare, even in the toughest gigs. Most of this kind of stuff usually happens outside or away from the venue, although *occasionally* it does boil over inside and it can happen while you're on stage.

In larger venues, fights are usually isolated incidents that flare up in seconds and disappear just as quickly. The all-out pub brawl like you see in the movies is, thankfully, very rare indeed.

I did once see a guy get punched so hard that he went to the ground incredibly fast. So fast in fact that his jeans completely split all the way up the sides on both legs. It seems like a gross exaggeration now but it really did happen. If they put that in a movie it would be dismissed as far-fetched, but I saw it with my own eyes.

With smaller issues you probably won't even be aware that something has occurred until it's over. Larger fights are unmistakeable. If this ever happens while you're on stage, despite what you see in the movies, stop what you're doing and get off stage. No explanation, no preamble, just stop what you're doing and get off.

Whatever happens next is a security issue and not something that you need to be involved in. The venue should then implement it's own policy for dealing with such issues. It is important that you don't make any kind of comment or take any action that could potentially involve you in the shenanigans taking place. Fights can be dangerous and there is no need for you to get involved in anything that happens.

I remember once waiting to go on in a tough club in the North of England. The evening seemed to be running late and I quickly got the feeling that something was wrong. Soon, the dressing room door opened and a guy walked in. He was in a panic. He explained that a huge fight was going on in the hall and that the police were on their way. He then counted the fee out onto the table and told me to get out as quickly as possible. I hadn't even done the show.

You see, it's not all bad news!

SOMEONE CLIMBS UP ON STAGE

If ever someone climbs up on stage unannounced, the solution is simple... STOP EVERYTHING, GET OFF STAGE AND MAKE SURE YOU TAKE THE MICROPHONE WITH YOU.

There is no need to begin a discussion about the issue at close quarters and in front of the rest of the audience. Just get off and let the organisers eject the idiot and regain control on your behalf.

Enough said.

THROWING THINGS

Discussion on his subject is very straightforward...

IF SOMEONE IS THROWING THINGS AT YOU ON STAGE...
GET OFF.

No messing, no questions, no statements, just get off. At no time should your personal safety be compromised while you are performing on stage.

If someone throws something on stage, be it as small as a beer mat, or as large as an elephant, no matter what it is...

- **STOP WHAT YOU'RE DOING**

- **SAY NOTHING**

- **PUT THE MICROPHONE BACK IN THE STAND**

- **EXIT THE STAGE**

Inform the Compère, Entertainments Manager, Security Official, Owner or the appropriate responsible individual over what has happened and allow them to sort it for you.

Don't get into a discussion about it while you're on stage, just stop what you're doing and get out of the way, in silence. You should not be tempted to respond in any way.

You will not have the time or the ability to safely assess what is being thrown at you, or why.

It may be harmless but you will not know that at this stage. Nor will you know if the person who threw it is harmless or otherwise. You are entitled to a safe working environment when you are on stage. There is no need to continue your act under circumstances like this.

The organiser should take reasonable steps to provide you with that safety and they should also take reasonable steps to deal with any infringements of your personal security. The same is true for _all_ issues of personal safety while on stage.

Don't get locked into the idea that you somehow have to stand there and take it because '_the show must go on_'.

You don't and it doesn't.

ALWAYS MAKE SURE THAT YOU ARE SAFE WHEN YOU ARE ON STAGE.

IF THERE IS SERIOUS DOUBT...

GET OFF.

DYING ON STAGE AND GETTING BOOED OFF

This is without doubt every entertainer's worst nightmare. What we are talking about is the event of total rejection from a large section of the audience. 'Dying' on stage happens every now and again to all professional performers, but being 'booed off' is extremely rare. I have only ever seen it a couple of times. For the sake of completeness let's discuss what happens, why it happens and how you might handle getting 'booed off'.

Experiencing any kind of rejection from an audience can be soul-destroying. Most of the time, any rejection that you do experience will come in the form of indifference... They will just ignore you, start talking and forget that you exist.

ACTUALLY GETTING 'BOOED OFF' STAGE IS VERY RARE.

With the advent of TV talent shows televising their audition processes, we have seen more than a lifetime's worth of acts getting booed off on Television recently. In a live situation it is rare.

It tends not to happen as much to singers and other entertainers as it does comedians and comedy performers. The reason is that it is easier to be indifferent to what a singer is doing, whereas a comedian requires your full attention and cannot work without it. It is possible for a singer to sing in the background whereas a comedian does not have this option – If the audience aren't listening, they aren't laughing. A comedian is also much more intrusive if he's not playing for laughs. The audience will want to shut him up if they're not paying attention. He/she just becomes an unnecessary irritation, unlike background music which is tolerable.

Opinions on subjects like being booed off are always going to be divided. There will be many that wish to make judgement over why a performer is booed off in the first place, whether they deserved it and so on.

I heard recently of an event where a comedian was first slow hand-clapped then booed off stage by an audience largely made up of other performers.

The comedian in question was a well established entertainer with many years of experience under his belt. On the night it just went horribly wrong for him and the audience began to slow hand-clap while he was working. He defied them and continued with his act. As they began to boo him he explained that he was a good comedian and would not be put off. *Eventually* he gave in and left the stage.

Personally, I couldn't see why the audience had harassed him in this way. The organisers must have seen his act before they booked him and they must have thought it was suitable for their event. The comic was only doing the act he'd been booked to do so if that turned out to be unsuitable for their audience, that's not his fault. That's his act.

The reason that they gave him such a hard time is that most of the audience had never stood in the comedian's shoes. They had never experienced that kind of rejection for themselves. They may have been performers, but most of them were amateur performers and they certainly weren't comedians. The comedian was booked to do his act, which he did.

After the event, several internet forums were running discussion threads on the issue and many people were justifying their choice to 'boo off' the performer. So, one thing is for certain... Some people feel that it is their <u>right</u> to *boo someone off* if they don't like them. For our purposes let's dispense with the reasons why, ignore any justifications and simply acknowledge that it can happen... for whatever reason.

The most common cause of being *booed off* is usually not the fault of the act. It is often (as in this case) the fault of the booker or the agent who has provided the wrong kind of entertainment for a particular occasion. Most agents book with caution, but some don't. I have been booked *'blind'* many times (that's where the agent hasn't seen the act personally). It can be a risky business for all concerned.

Now I know that there will be a few *experts* out there who will say that an act should be able to adapt according to the circumstances and all that kind of stuff. The reality is that most acts *do* adapt, to an extent, but most good performers are specialists in one particular field. They tend to be very good at one thing, that's what they are known for, that's what they stick to and that's what their audiences expect.

Conversely it is also true that some performers have a number of skills, but they are rarely *specialists* in more than one area.

It's comparable to booking a plumber to come and fix the pipes and then complaining when they can't fix the electrics. It's madness, but this kind of thing often happens to entertainers. You can be booked to do what you normally do and then receive a complaint when it's not right for their event. How could *you* know that in advance if you don't know the clientèle? You have to trust the booker's judgement.

Remember that not all acts are suitable for all events... It is certainly not a one-size-fits-all situation. Once you arrive at a venue where the requirements are beyond your capabilities, it's too late. You're faced with two choices: Go on and try your luck or let the client down.

Dependent on your experience, it is possible to turn a job around and get a result, but don't expect this to happen in all cases. The odds will be heavily stacked against you. A young trendy 'new-school' observational comic is always going to struggle at the Old Folks tea party. Conversely a 50-something 'old school' gag teller is going to get a hard time in an 18-30's city centre nightclub. Fact.

Their material just isn't geared for the audience that they are facing. They may quickly search their minds for more suitable material but it won't be long before the cracks begin to show.

Nonetheless, entertainers can be booked into inappropriate venues if the agent or the booker doesn't know the act or the individual requirements of the venue and/or clientèle.

On occasions the booker may have no knowledge of the entertainment business at all! Remember that comedians come in all shapes and sizes. So do singers, magicians and pretty much every other kind of entertainer you might mention. It's all a matter of matching the act to the clientèle. If that doesn't happen then you're in it up to your neck and you're going to need something special to get you out of it.

There'll be plenty of advice out there, but most of it will be next to useless in the real world. Most people will be able to offer you an opinion on how you should handle this.

As with my earlier example about the comic who was booed off, there was plenty of online opinion about what he should or shouldn't have done – all offered by people who had little or no real knowledge of his business or his situation.

The only thing that I read on the incident that had any real credibility to it was written by another pro comic. What he said was: *'His only mistake was not knowing when he was beaten...'*

On the subject of opinions and advice, I remember once sitting in a dressing room waiting to go on at a club and I started to read the graffiti on the walls. Most of it was an account of who had *'died'* on stage there. There were a few *'R.I.P.'s'*, a few arrows pointing towards the stage bearing the words *'This way to the lions'* and lots of *'abandon all hope...'* sort of messages. Underneath all this was a paragraph of writing which went something like: *'If you give it 100% and connect with your audience, they will respect you in return and give you the attention you desire...'* etc. The entire statement was extolling the virtues of working hard to gain the attention of the audience against the odds. At the end of this diatribe, right at the bottom of the wall, someone else had written...

'Obviously new to the game...'

...No, it wasn't me, but I confess I wish I 'd have thought of it.

In the course of a booking there can often be a string of agents involved, all of which increase the distance between the act and the actual booker. The reality is that while the agent always wants to do a good job, they're not the one who has to actually stand there and do the show. The agent will usually care more about the client's reaction than the situation from your point of view, particularly if the event/act is <u>un</u>successful.

Remember also that an agent may have a number of acts out working that evening.

Some agents will even take the view that if one act out of the twenty has a bad night, well, it's not a bad record, eh? The worst that will happen to the agent is that they'll get a grade 6 b*llocking from the client on Monday morning and the agent can then just blame the act.

Sadly, it happens.

I have seen an agent stand at the back of a room and then make a discreet but speedy exit when the act was beginning to struggle on stage. I've seen it more than once.

The moral of the story is... When it all turns to sh*t don't automatically expect the agent to back you up. Some will, most won't. They will have the client's potential future bookings in mind and they can always do *them* without you. It is also worth noting that you should never call an agent on a Monday. Their phones are often jammed with complaining bookers and other agents who have used their acts over the weekend and now want to vent their spleen. Most agents are guaranteed to be in their worst moods on Monday mornings.

It is also important to point out that some agents are *very* conscientious and take great care in selecting just the right acts for their venues. Not all agents are bad and some will be *very* cautious about booking unseen acts or acts that may not perfectly suited to their venues. If all agents were like that, you wouldn't need this book and I would have nothing to write about.

Accepting the fact that you can be booked into the 'wrong' type of venue is really part of the professionals mindset. Most *'pros'* can shrug off the occasional failure, but that comes with time. The reason they can do it is because they know that they have performed their act hundreds (or thousands) of times and *'killed'* (had a great show) with it. The fact that once in a while it doesn't work is tempered by the fact that it has worked for them so many times in the past that they know not to blame themselves for the occasional blip. The 'bad show' is often more a case of bad booking... Though not always.

If you find yourself in a situation where you're getting *booed off*, or at least getting a really hard time from an audience, then the first thing you have to consider is whether you can do anything about it or not. It's time to weigh up the odds and consider accepting your fate.

Under these kinds of circumstances it is time to contemplate the thing that many professional entertainers just don't want to talk about...

Failure.

Despite what they may want to admit (or deny), most well-established TV comedians, professional entertainers and household names have all had to walk off stage having failed to raise a smile. It happens to every comic in the world at one time or another. I have seen this happen to many 'name' comedians. Most of them are still fearful of it happening – Particularly after a good spell of fame and success. Often they are in a comfortable enough position to choose their dates and venues wisely, rejecting potentially unsuitable dates and thereby ensuring that only the most suitable dates and venues actually go into the diary.

Most comics bury the experience of 'dying' in a dark corner of their minds, never to be relived, some of them deny it, but rest assured they have all been there.

So what can we do if we ever find ourselves in a situation where we're really getting 'booed off'?

Well, like our earlier example, one of the key considerations has to be the acceptance of knowing when you're beaten. If you weigh up the odds and you realise that this is the case... That you truly are beaten... then it's time to get off.

If you're getting booed off - for whatever reason - then weigh up the odds quickly. Here's how the thought process goes:

- **IS THE SITUATION SALVAGEABLE?**

- **CAN I MAKE CHANGES THAT WILL MAKE A DIFFERENCE?**

- **IF YOU CAN MAKE CHANGES, IMPLEMENT THEM QUICKLY.**

- **IF THE CHANGES HAVE NO EFFECT OR YOU HAVE NONE TO MAKE... GET OFF.**

It is important to reiterate that leaving the stage is a last resort. If you can salvage the situation, do! Leaving the stage may mean that you have to argue for any fees due to you as you have not done what you are contracted to do.

To counteract this you may want to have a clause in your contract that ensures that the client should ensure reasonable order in the room before you perform – or they pay you before you go on. This is a matter entirely for your own consideration.

My *opinion* is that if the comedian fails to make the audience laugh and as a result walks off stage early then that is his own fault.

If the comedian is unable to perform his act because the room is unruly or hostile then that's *not* his fault... Unless of course he created the hostility. But, like I said, that's only my opinion. If the comedian is performing his regular material and *that* is unsuitable for the venue, then that is not the comedian's fault, it is the booker's fault: The booker has booked the act to perform 'as known' and comedian has attempted to perform his regular act. You may have to argue that one out with them if it's not written down anywhere.

Remember that you don't always have to stand-and-deliver in the face of extreme adversity.

I have seen comedians continue under such circumstances and the result is that the evening just deteriorates rapidly. The audience (and probably the booker) won't thank you for it.

Often, if you're struggling, a booker will want you to get off as soon as possible so that they can salvage the evening with something else. Under such circumstances 'staying on' can be counter-productive. This is a rare situation but it does happen occasionally.

In truth, getting booed off is more likely to happen at the beginning of a performer's career. This is due to a number of factors: Material, experience, ability, reputation and lots more. Someone who is just starting out is more likely to still be experimenting with unproven material. Once they find their style and find out what works for them they'll most likely stick to that and reduce the incidence of failure. Nonetheless, failures do happen, even to experienced comics, and there is no way of knowing which way a gig will go until you get on stage. You may find that certain times of year affect how well your act goes. The amount of time your audience have been drinking, or how long they have been waiting can also have an effect.

You may find that if you're performing shows over a long holiday weekend, like Easter for example, the shows can be harder. People will often 'pace' their social lives when there are several holiday days all together. They'll often drink and party more on the first day of the holidays, pace themselves for a few days then start early on the last day and be drunk and incoherent by lunchtime. By the evening of the last day the venue often has only two kinds of people in it: Drunks and stragglers. All of which will, of course, affect your show.

If an audience have been sitting in a cold, silent auditorium for a considerable length of time before the show starts they can be hard work. Poor weather can have a similar effect too. There are many factors that can affect your chances of success before you even step on the stage. It is not always just a 'bad' act.

In conclusion, all comedians *die* at some point but very few ever get booed off. Most performers will never experience it as it is very, very rare... But that doesn't stop most performers from being in fear of it.

The worst that will normally happen is that the audience will ignore you – you will know what they're thinking – and that will be enough. You'll do the rest of the damage to yourself, just by thinking about it. If the worst does happen, don't fight against them, don't defy them and don't antagonise them. Take a hint and get off.

GETTING BOOED ON

OK, I admit it's a slightly glib heading, but this *can* happen. Some audiences really are 'un-entertain-able'. There are also certain venues where the local sport is to give the act a hard time. I have also known it happen when a venue changes its entertainment policy after years of doing the same thing – I guess some people just don't like change!

In the UK there are many tales of acts getting a hard time when venues first started to get rid of live musicians. Venues started to book self-contained acts with their own PA systems and backing tracks. Many of the locals disliked the change and gave the acts a hard time.

For whatever reason, occasionally an audience may give you a less than enthusiastic 'welcome' to the stage.

If this happens to you, in truth, there's not really much you can do about it. Like the 'bad introduction' situation or the 'minutes silence' you need to have a big personality and a strong act to overcome this one. However, there are a few things that may help...

If the audience really starts to give you a hard time from the word go you might just stand there, remain silent and show no reaction while they heckle you. A good comeback from this is to then add the 'ventriloquist' line. I'm not entirely sure where this came from originally but I have heard a few people lay claim to its origination. It has been around quite a few years in various forms and I've heard a number of comics use it in all sorts of circumstances. Basically what you do is allow the heckles to come in and then, after a short while, say:

"I'm actually a ventriloquist and I do all my own heckling..."

If you want you can follow up with:

"I can also do it while drinking a glass of water..."

If you have a glass or a bottle of water, drink it. If somebody heckles again you say: 'I did that'. If they don't heckle you again then you have just managed to shut them up and now you can get on with your act. You don't actually *need* to have a glass of water to do the line anyway.

Other reactions to might give are:

"Thanks for the welcome! I've been booed off a few times but that's the first time I can recall being booed 'on'"

OR

"Thank you very much. Your disapproval is more than justified..."

There are many lines that you can adapt for this eventuality. Have a look at lines that cover 'lack of applause', these will give you plenty of inspiration. You can always modify a line to suit your purpose. A few tweaks here and there and you've got a new line! That is how most ad-libbing is achieved.

POWER CUTS AND VOLUME METERS

These are the bane of every entertainer's life. If you've not experienced one then let me explain... The volume meter is becoming increasingly common in venues that stand close to housing developments. If the local authority receives a number of complaints about noise pollution from those living locally then they can insist in a volume meter being installed in a venue. The volume meter unceremoniously cuts the power if a certain volume level is exceeded.

For those doing speech based entertainment this is rarely an issue, but occasionally a loud yell into the microphone is enough to cut you off for 60 seconds until the power comes back on.

Make sure that you know about these things in advance... Weeks in advance if possible. The reason for this is that volume meters can damage audio equipment by simply cutting the power. If you use your own PA equipment you need to know if one of these is in use. If you haven't been informed in advance that the venue uses one and you are concerned about the safety of your equipment, ask the venue to indemnify it against damage. A sharp cut in power is particularly harmful to the HF units (tweeters) in any speakers you may be using.

A quick fix on the night is to ask the venue to plug you into an uninterrupted supply, while you agree to follow the meter. The meter usually has a display on the wall showing acceptable levels. This will allow you to follow the meter and make adjustments to the levels without running the risk of damage to your equipment if the meter is a little 'trigger happy'. The meter is only ever rigged to a certain number of circuits on the stage. The rest of the building will be on a uninterrupted supply.

One thing is for sure... It won't interrupt the power supply to the beer pumps or the gaming machines.

If the power does go off while you're on stage there is little that you can say that will actually get a laugh because the microphone will go off too. You might stand there and mime doing the act in sign language or step forward, cup your hands around your mouth and shout really loud...

"THERE WAS AN ENGLISHMAN, AN IRISHMAN AND A SCOTSMAN...!"

...As if you're attempting to tell a joke. The only problem is that you have no way of doing any other real lines as nobody will be able to hear you.

There was a time when every other venue seemed to have one of these things. At that time I carried a megaphone in my bag and used to grab it when the power went off. I did various gags with it to fill the time till the power came back on.

My favourite was a variation on an old clown skit. What I did was point the megaphone at the floor whilst acting as if attempting to turn it on. Then I would switch it on and make it give a great burst of feedback. Putting it to my mouth to speak I would then switch it off and start talking. Obviously there was no sound coming out. Now, apparently realising it had gone off again I would repeat the routine until it finally came on really loud. It played for good laughs and filled the time till the power came back on.

These days volume meters seem rarer, or perhaps I'm just not playing those venues any more?

In any case, make sure that you ask the booker if the venue has one of these when you take the booking. It should be stated on the contract and you should be made aware of it well in advance of the performance.

AGGRESSIVE PERSON SPOILING FOR A FIGHT

Occasionally I have had to deal with someone who was just spoiling for a fight. Thankfully it's not something I have had to deal with too often but most comics get it from time to time. Depending on the kind of act you do, you'll get more or less of your fair share of idiots. Stage comics tend to get the lion's share of these numbskulls.

The key to dealing with them is to make sure that the rest of the room is on your side. You'll already have been through the first few steps of the drill: Ignoring the first heckle, asking them to repeat it, then using a few mild put-downs. If all this escalates quickly into a confrontational situation you'll need to act fast and think even faster. Your reaction needs to be similar to the one we discussed for dealing with drunks, unless of course you happen to be a martial arts expert.

Once you've tried a few put downs and got the measure of the guy, it should quickly become clear whether the guy is going to back down or not. If he isn't and he's becoming aggressive, threatening you or generally overstepping the mark, don't be afraid to ask for help.

By now the venue officials should have spotted the troublemaker and they should be taking steps to eject him from the premises. If they're not taking steps to sort the issue, you'll need to remind them in very clear terms from the stage. Read again through the 'Drunk Heckler' section on page 27. This will give you more information on how to deal with people who are out of control.

Remember if all else fails and things turn sour, make your exit. Get off stage and let someone sort the problem out for you. Crowd control issues are not the responsibility of entertainers.

If there are security personnel on duty they may need to know that there *really is* something wrong and that it's not all part of the act. Inform them about any trouble as soon as you can. I have heard the phrase *"I thought it was all part of the act"* too many times. It is amazing how many times someone was (allegedly) *"just about to step in"* before I've ended up having to sort the problem out for myself.

If there *is* a serious problem, make it clear and let someone know before it gets out of hand.

THE POST-SHOW CRITIC

This is one of those situations you may encounter from time to time and it can be difficult to follow the advice here, *but please do*, it will save you a lot of time and grief in the long run.

The *post-show critic* comes in all shapes and sizes but they usually emerge from what seem like fairly innocuous conversations after the show. The critic has a *'bee in his bonnet'* and wants to let you know all about it... And they've usually had a drink or two as well. The conversation usually goes something like: *'You shouldn't have done that'* or *'you should have said this'* or *'I liked this about your act but I thought that bit was rubbish'*. The actual content of the conversation is irrelevant, the guy is just spoiling for an argument.

The *post-show critic* usually emerges after you've had a really good night. The rest of the audience have enjoyed your show but this idiot thinks he knows better and he's going to tell you all about what you should and shouldn't have done. No matter what he says, take a hint...

SAY GOODNIGHT AND WALK AWAY FROM IDIOTS

The guy has nothing valid to say and is just wanting to spoil your evening, so just walk away. It can be frustrating and you may want to discuss the guy's apparent disappointment with your act, but it's an argument that you cannot win. The game is rigged against you and so it's best to just slip away quietly. My favourite technique is to politely put the guy 'on hold' for a moment, pop back to the dressing room and look as if I just remembered I'm looking for something, then a few minutes later, bid everyone a good night and exit as if I forgot him during the distractions.

This may seem a little ignorant but once you spot what's going on (you'll soon learn to identify the signs) you're better off leaving quietly than you are standing and arguing your case. If you act out the return visit to the dressing room convincingly it should look like you genuinely forgot him. You'll save yourself a lot of grief by doing so.

Arguing your case with this guy doesn't get you anywhere in these situations. If you don't believe me, give it a go.

You'll just get home later than normal, achieve nothing and the guy will *still* think that you're an idiot. It's easier to accept that occasionally some people will not enjoy your success on a good night.

Instead they'll want to knock you down a peg or two and share with you the benefit of their inexperience. With the wrong kind of person these situations can become inflamed into aggressive arguments and even fights so it's better to just agree and walk away.

I remember once arguing with a guy after a show in Sheffield. Sheffield is notoriously difficult for comics and on this night I'd finished the show and done really well. The booker was over the moon, the audience were generous in their appreciation and the venue staff were lauding on the praise too... A good night. Then along comes the *post-show critic*, every inch a d*ckhead.

I stopped for a few moments chat with some people in the audience and Mr Critic volunteers himself to give me a run-down of what he didn't like. It starts, as they always do, with a compliment... *'I thought your act was great... BUT...'*. Then he goes on to tell me what he thought was wrong, what I should have done and so on. Don't get me wrong here, I'm not adverse to a bit of constructive criticism, I think that is always useful and I've benefited a lot from it. This is different. This is all about making you feel small and criticising something that worked well. It is a form of social jealousy.

The fact that I'd actually performed for double the time they had booked me for and (on top of that) I'd done it for half my usual fee was irrelevant, he wanted his say. I remember trying to explain everything in reasonable terms but the goal posts kept on moving. My simple reply should have been...

"Oh I'm sorry you didn't like it, still better luck next time, eh?"

And then I should have gone home. But I didn't. I stayed and tried to explain myself in polite terms... And I regretted it. You can't win against these idiots so just cut your losses and leave as politely as you can. Arguing or explaining is time-consuming and pointless. Make the smart move and put the whole situation to bed as soon as you can.

You'll be glad you did.

THE POST-SCRIPT

Well folks, our journey is almost over. I hope that you have enjoyed our meanderings through the world of theatrical disaster...

Seriously, I do hope that you have picked up a few tips that will be useful along the way. Understand too that it is difficult to give any guidance aimed specifically at you and your individual style within these pages. I have had to generalise, at least some of the time.

There will be many kinds of performer using this book – Some may be lucky enough to never need to use a word of it, others will use it every time they set foot on the stage. I have tried to include stuff that is of use to everybody and I hope that Includes you.

There may be things here that you can't see any real use for, but rest assured, somebody somewhere will most definitely find them essential. Like I said at the start, if there are things in here that are not of use to you, then thank your lucky stars that it's one interruption that is not affecting your show. Spare a thought too for the poor soul who has to deal with it day-in-day-out.

If you have any specific comments or questions you can go to www.hecklertactics.com for the answers. Here, you can pass on any specific stories about using this material and you can also share your favourite put-down lines. There is a section of FAQ's too, which are there to help you. You can also let me know if there's something you think I should have included here, but haven't yet. Check it out.

So now I wish you every success with your act and trust that, from here on in, when it comes to nailing hecklers to the wall, you'll be more than prepared...

Good luck!

James Brandon.

NOTES